My Forbidden Face

My Forbidden Face

GROWING UP UNDER THE TALIBAN: A Young Woman's Story

LATIFA

Written with the collaboration of Shekeba Hachemi

Translated by Linda Coverdale

talk miramax books

HYPERION

NEW YORK

Translation by Linda Coverdale
International Rights Management Susanna Lea Associates

Printed in the United States of America. For information address: Hyperion, 77 W. 66th Street, New York, New York 10023-6298.

ISBN: 1-4013-5925-6

First edition

10 9 8 7 6

Life always comes to an end
There is no need to submit
If my life means submission
I do not need that life
In slavery
It can rain drops of gold
Then I say to the sky
I do not need that rain

This book records past and recent events experienced by my family in my country, Afghanistan.

I hope it will serve as a key to other women, those whose words are locked away, those who have hidden what they have witnessed in their hearts and in their memories. I dedicate it to all the Afghan girls and women who have kept their dignity until their last breath. To all those, deprived of their rights in their own country, who live in darkness even after the dawn of the twenty-first century. To all those women executed in public before the eyes of their children and loved ones, without pity, or justice.

I offer it also to my mother, who has helped me every moment by giving me lessons in freedom and resistance.

Latifa

Contents

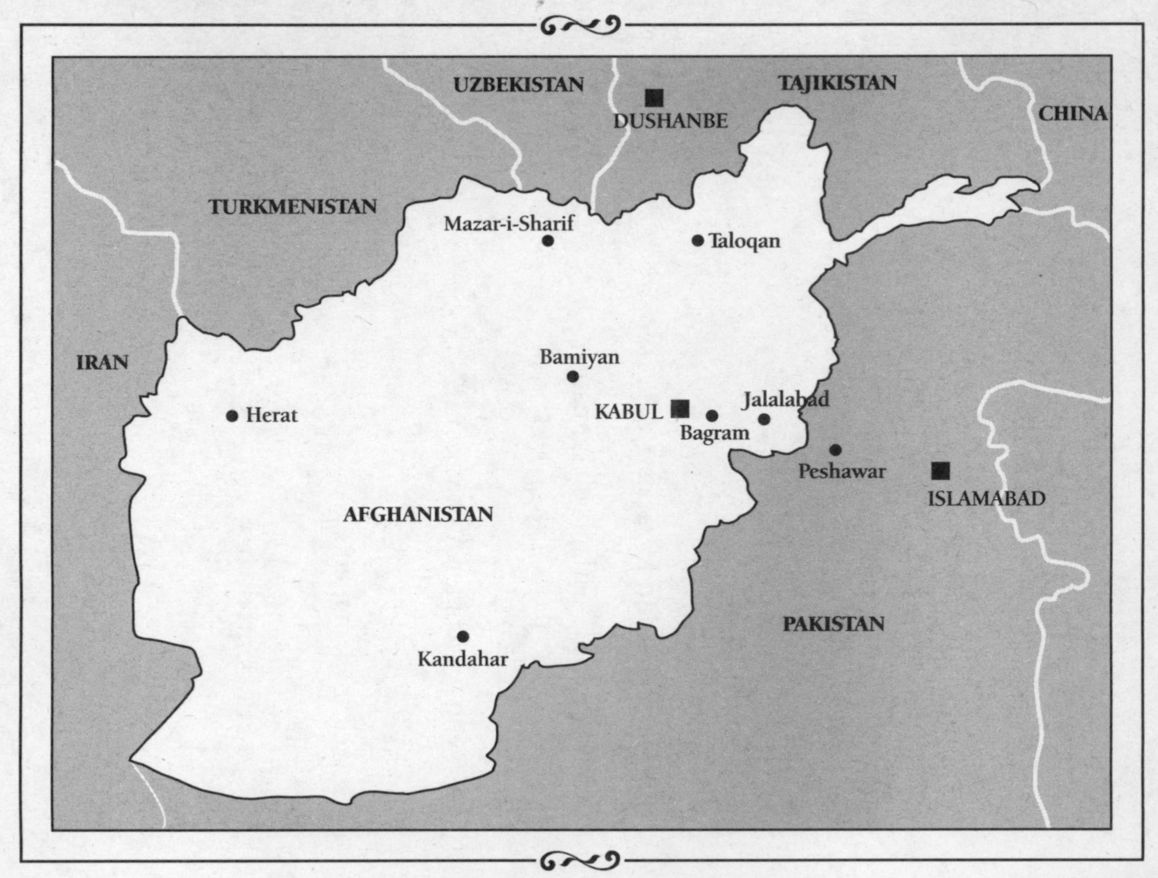
UZBEKISTAN
DUSHANBE
TAJIKISTAN
CHINA
TURKMENISTAN
Mazar-i-Sharif
Taloqan
IRAN
Bamiyan
Herat
KABUL
Bagram
Jalalabad
Peshawar
ISLAMABAD
AFGHANISTAN
PAKISTAN
Kandahar

Preface

Since holy war came to Manhattan, the West has become used to talk of fatwas and mullahs, the Pashtun and the mujahideen. But as we digest news reports and public statements, there is a growing hunger for more intimate knowledge of the mind-set and experience of the Afghan people. *My Forbidden Face* carries the voice of a young girl coming of age under the terror of the Taliban and reveals the complicated touchpoints between our world and hers.

Latifa, writing under a pseudonym because she fears for her friends and family still in Afghanistan, recounts how the politics of her homeland have intruded upon every aspect of her young life—from the Soviet troops who conscripted and then imprisoned her brother, to the dueling massacres by the warlord Hekmatyar and General Massoud that interrupted her studies and her sister's wedding, to the terrifying day that the white flag of the Taliban was first flown over Kabul.

That was the day when Latifa went to the town square to see the mutilated body of a former president and then became a prisoner in her own home. The radio that once played poetry and foreign news now blasted chanted decrees: no music, no pets, no whistling, no makeup, and of course, virtual house arrest for women. Women were only allowed to leave home when accompanied by a male relative and dressed in the full chadri. Latifa went from studying journalism and editing a cultural magazine to the "morbid inertia" of knowing that she was forbidden to learn, create, or work. The familiar pleasures of her everyday life—posters of Brooke Shields and Elvis, sweatpants and running shoes, photos of her mother as a girl, even the family dog—were all suddenly high crimes. Kabul's sports stadium became a public execution ground. Latifa became hostage and witness to the barbaric acts that the Taliban used to keep its grip on Kabul.

In our country, young people are infamously detached from politics, with the large majority preferring to keep more than an arm's length from the voting booth or the soapbox. For this young girl, all of the personal is political—every aspect of her future depends on the posture of Afghan politicians, and the nuances of various factions are matters of life and death. Latifa gathers information by listening secretly to the BBC and paying careful attention to the word on the streets of Kabul: rumors, slang, political gossip, and terrifying stories of state action.

Throughout the book, Latifa also reveals the complex American influence in Kabul, from her crush on Leonardo DiCaprio to her belief that the Taliban came with the blessing and might of the United States. Latifa's community had enough contact with Western popular culture and political ideals to be left with a stinging feeling of hypocritical abandonment when the world turned a blind eye to Taliban oppression. "Even Afghans living abroad couldn't care less!" cries her brother. Latifa's teenage impressions of American foreign policy, the United Nations, and the legacy of Osama bin Laden challenge Americans to learn more about our own actions abroad and try to understand the perspective of a culture that is not as distant as it once seemed.

This story is also one of a young woman finding her own voice and claiming her sense of self, even as it is officially denied her. As if confiding in a diary or a close friend, Latifa muses about how traditional a wife she might be; what her mother's deep depression means for her own professional dreams; and how the Taliban's decrees distort her own reading of the Koran. Carolyn Heilbrun has written that "power is the ability to take one's place in whatever discourse is essential to action and the right to have one's part matter." In that sense, *My Forbidden Face* is about a single young woman seizing power from the Taliban and cherishing hope for a day when all women of her homeland will be free. If the events of September 11 lead to the Western world's awareness of and dedication to that goal, then the Afghan saying that Latifa and her family relied on will ring true: "Joy and sorrow are sisters."

Karenna Gore Schiff
December 2001

ONE

The White Flag Over the Mosque

9 A.M., September 27, 1996. Someone knocks violently on our door. My whole family has been on edge since dawn, and now we all start in alarm. My father jumps up to see who it is while my mother looks on anxiously, haggard with exhaustion after a sleepless night. None of us got any sleep: The rocket fire around the city didn't let up until two in the morning. My sister Soraya and I kept whispering in the dark; even after things quieted down, we couldn't fall asleep. And yet here in Kabul, we're used to being the target of rocket fire. I'm only sixteen years old, but I feel as though I've been hearing that din all my life. The city has been surrounded and bombarded for so long, the smoke and flames of the murderous fighting have terrified us so often, sometimes even sending us

rushing down to the basement, that another night in this racket is just part of our daily routine!

Until this morning.

Papa returns to the kitchen, followed by Farad, our young cousin, who is pale and breathless. He seems to be shaking inside, and his face is taut with fear. He can hardly speak, stammering out words in a series of strange gasps.

"I came . . . to find out how you were. Are you all right? You haven't seen anything? You don't know? But they're here! They've taken Kabul! The Taliban are in Kabul. They haven't come to your place yet? They haven't demanded that you hand over any weapons?"

"No, no one's been here, but we saw the white flag waving over the mosque—Daoud spotted it a few hours ago. We were afraid the worst had happened. . . ."

This morning, around five o'clock, my young brother Daoud went downstairs as usual to fetch some water from the tap in the courtyard of our building, but came hurrying back up with the basin still empty.

"I saw a white flag over the mosque and another one over the school."

The flag of the Taliban. It had never before flown over Kabul. I had seen it only on television or in newspaper photographs.

We knew the Taliban were not far away; people in the city kept saying they were five or ten miles from the capital, but no one truly believed they would manage to enter Kabul. When we quickly turn on the radio and the television to hear some news, there is still nothing, the same dreadful nothing—no sound or picture, nothing since six o'clock yesterday afternoon. This morning my father also tried to reach the rest of the family in Kabul, but the telephone is still dead as well.

I fiddle nervously with the dial of our battery-powered radio, searching through the static. No trace of our local station, Radio Kabul, or the BBC, or the Voice of America, which I try looking for at that unlikely hour, just on the off chance. . . . If Farad hadn't risked racing over a mile on his bike from his neighborhood to ours, we wouldn't have had any information, nothing but the undeniable presence of those white flags.

What Farad has seen is so frightening, so appalling, that he blurts it out all at once.

"They've hanged Najibullah and his brother, on Aryana Square. . . . It's horrible! Horrible!"

He turns back and forth from my father to Daoud as he speaks, then gazes at my sister and me in anguish. We've heard terrible things about what the Taliban do to women in the provinces they already occupy. I've never seen Farad in such a panic, never seen such overwhelming fear in his eyes.

"Can you imagine? Najibullah. They've strung him up with plastic tubing! There's a big crowd, the Taliban are making everyone look at the bodies, they're beating people. I saw them."

Petrified, the five of us are speechless.

Even after my brother told us he'd seen the white flags, I didn't want to believe the truth. The government forces must have pulled back to prepare for another attack on the Taliban, or else they've taken refuge more to the north, in a suburb of the city. The mujahideen can't have abandoned Kabul. So many times I've heard, read, and preferred to ignore what the government has been telling us about the Taliban: "They imprison women in their own homes. They prevent them from working, from going to school. Women have no more lives, the Taliban take away their daughters, burn the villagers' houses, force the men to join their army. They want to destroy the country!"

Just yesterday, despite the civil war, life was "normal" in Kabul, even though the city is in ruins. Yesterday I went to the seamstress with my sister to try on the dresses we were going to wear to a wedding today. There would have been music, we would have danced. Life can't stop like this on the twenty-seventh of September in 1996. I'm only sixteen and still have so many things to do—I have to pass the entrance examination to study journalism at the university. . . . No, it's impossible that the Taliban could remain in Kabul; it's just a temporary setback.

I hear my father talking with Daoud, but I'm so upset I catch only scraps of their conversation.

"Najibullah is a Pashtun, like they are—it's crazy for them to turn on a Pashtun. And they arrested him in the UN compound? They hanged him? That doesn't make any sense."

My father is also a Pashtun, the dominant ethnic group in the country. Like many others, he had thought that if through some misfortune the Taliban managed to invade the capital, they would certainly seek out Najibullah, not to hang him, but to set him free and invite him to join their new government.

Kabulis don't much care for Najibullah, a former leader of our government and a man capable of switching sides as easily as arms and drug traffickers move across the borders of Pakistan. My father is very critical of him and thinks he is a traitor to our country. Corrupt and criminal, Najibullah directed the Afghan Communist secret police, the Khad,* a sinister clone of the Soviet KGB. During the last coup d'état, in April 1992, when the resistance besieged Kabul, he simply ran away. Army troops caught him at the airport just as he was about to board a plane to escape abroad. When they forced him

*In December 1979 the Soviet Union invaded Afghanistan, executed President Hafizullah Amin, replaced him with Babrak Karmal, and established the Khad, which began purges that killed an estimated 80,000 people. [translator's note]

to stay, he took refuge at the UN compound near Aryana Square, and there he remained until today.

I was only a child when he made a speech calling for reconciliation among the various factions of the resistance, a speech he gave on the very square where Farad saw him hanging. If the Taliban are capable of hunting down an ex-president even in the UN headquarters in Kabul, then terror and chaos have taken over indeed.

Still shaken, my cousin Farad doesn't want to stay away from home too long.

"If you must go out, be very careful, Uncle. I've seen some of them flogging people with big whips! They're scary, they dress like Pakistanis in long, loose pants, they drive around in four-by-fours and stop to beat people for no reason. . . . Sometimes they attack men who don't wear beards. And you have no beard!"

Farad doesn't have a beard, either. Do you grow a beard at age sixteen when you wear running shoes and jeans? When you listen to rock music and daydream over sentimental Indian novels, like lots of boys his age?

The Taliban are all bearded. Their edict specifies that men must wear beards as long as a man's hand. They never wear the *pakol,* the traditional Afghan cap that has become an emblem of the resistance. Besides, we know they're not all Pashtuns, or even Afghans: They're supported by Pakistan, and they recruit followers abroad. Footage on television and eyewitnesses from the provinces they control prove that their ranks include many Pakistanis, as well as Arabs from Muslim countries, most of whom don't even speak our language.

My father checks the street from the balcony of our apartment. The neighborhood is rather quiet; the Taliban flag still waves atop the mosque. But our minds are reeling. We look at one another, dumbfounded. Farad gulps down a glass of hot tea. Papa comes in from the balcony, shaking his head: He simply cannot believe the Taliban have hanged Najibullah.

This morning, my father and I will not be going jogging with Bingo, our dog. This morning, my father is silently wondering about a thousand things he keeps to himself so as not to distress our mother any further. She has already been sorely tried by seventeen years of war. War, fighting—that's all I've ever known since I was born on March 20, 1980, the first day of spring. But even under the Soviets, even under the rocket fire of the feuding military factions, even in the ruins, we were still living in relative freedom in Kabul.

What kind of life will our father be able to offer his loved ones? What will happen to his children? I was lucky to be born into a united and affectionate family, one both liberal and religious. My oldest brother, Wahid, lives in Russia. My oldest sister, Shakila, is married and lives with her in-laws, following the custom of our people. She's in Pakistan, waiting to join her husband in the United

States. Soraya, who is twenty, is unmarried and has been a flight attendant for Aryana Afghan Airlines for three years now. She came home two days ago from a routine trip to Dubai and was to have left again this morning. Daoud is studying economics. I just passed the first part of a university entrance examination to study journalism. That has always been my dream. My father and everyone else in my family hope to see me complete my studies and become a reporter, traveling around the country, earning my living. Will all this come to an end in a single moment?

I need to see what's going on in Aryana Square, and so does my sister. We want to convince ourselves that the Taliban are really here, that they've really hanged Najibullah and his brother, that the catastrophe I refused to believe in only yesterday has actually happened to us. My brother Wahid, who was a soldier during the Soviet occupation and then a resistance fighter under General Massoud, always used to say about the Taliban, who were moving up from the south, "You can't imagine the kind of foreign support they have. No one in Kabul has the slightest clue: They're powerful, they've got modern equipment—the government will never be able to stand up to those people."

At the time, we thought he was being too pessimistic. Now we realize that he was right. So to convince myself of this new reality, I want to see these Taliban soldiers with my own eyes.

My father has the same idea. Daoud will stay with Mama, who is too fragile to see such things, and the rest of us will drive to Aryana Square. Before taking off on his bike, a sturdy Chinese model, Farad warns my father once again:

"You should stay home! It would be safer."

But we must see this incredible sight. If I were already a reporter, it would be my duty to go to the square. I've never seen Najibullah, except for a few times on television, and I was so young then. People had been saying lately that he was writing an autobiography, which I was eager to read. Even those who betrayed our country, who supported the Soviets, are part of our recent history. Anyone who wants to be a journalist must learn everything, understand everything, know everything.

I usually wear sweatpants, a polo shirt or a pullover, and running shoes, but today Soraya and I dress prudently in long dresses and chadors, which we wear at home when we pray. Papa goes to get the car, which is parked near the local mosque. Carrying his bicycle on his shoulder, Farad follows us downstairs, where we wait for Papa, who soon drives up.

A neighbor calls to us.

"Have you heard? It seems they've hanged Najibullah on Aryana Square. What do you think of that?"

My father signals us discreetly to be cautious. In Kabul, and even in our neighborhood of Mikrorayan, you never know with whom you're dealing. The four modern housing complexes that make up this eastern section of the capital were built by the Soviets and form a kind of concrete village, with its big numbered apartment blocks, its business sector, its school. Many important officials in the Afghan Communist Party lived there, in what were considered luxurious quarters that were more comfortable than traditional houses. Most of the residents are acquainted with one another, and we recognize this neighbor, of course, but who knows what side he's on this morning?

Soraya replies prudently, in her usual calm and pleasant manner.

"That's what we heard, too. We're going to see what's happening."

"My daughter would like to go with you."

Farad whispers to Soraya to refuse: "Better not take anyone else—you can never tell what might happen over there."

Farad has younger sisters and a sense of responsibility. The girl pleads with us to take her along, but the answer is no.

We drive off toward Aryana Square. Sitting in the back with Soraya, I think about the wedding we will not be attending. A few minutes ago, when I mentioned the dresses we were supposed to go get from the seamstress today, Mama snapped at me.

"Don't you understand what's happening, Latifa? And you're talking about picking up dresses!"

"Don't worry," my father assured me. "I'll get them later."

I'm well aware that I'm a teenager who is spoiled by her father and coddled by her sisters, and who has grown up in an atmosphere of freedom until now. School, college, Sundays at the swimming pool, expeditions with my girlfriends in search of music tapes, film videos, novels to read avidly in bed in the evening . . . How I hope the resistance forces haven't abandoned us to our fate.

Along the way, Papa stops the car when one of our friends, a pharmacist, waves to him in recognition. The pharmacist's brother holds an important position in the government.

"Where are you going? To Aryana Square? I'd advise against it."

"We want to see things for ourselves."

"Well, then, I'll tell you something later on, when you return. Be careful!"

The streets are less crowded than usual; we see men, but not many women. The faces I glimpse in passing are strained: People seem to be in shock. Everything seems calm, however. In fifteen minutes we reach the avenue that runs from the airport to Aryana Square, which is already clogged with cars. This great square is the modern center of the city. My father warns us that he's going to make a quick tour of the square and park farther along. We drive past the American Embassy, the television building, the headquarters of Aryana Afghan Airlines. None of their doors are open.

Soraya has tears in her eyes.

"Look, that's where I work! Maybe I'll never be able to come here again. Even the television building is closed. . . ."

The car turns a corner of the square by Peace Avenue, the site of the UN compound. Facing us is the Ministry of Defense, where General Massoud had his office. And there, across from the Hotel Aryana, the most luxurious in Kabul, reserved primarily for tourists and Western journalists, stands a kind of watchtower ordinarily used by the police guards on duty to keep an eye on the ministry. Two corpses are hanging from this improvised gallows. Papa advises us to look quickly because he's not going to drive around the square again.

"Take a good look at the faces, so we can be sure it really is Najibullah and his brother."

And it really is: side by side, former president Najibullah, in traditional Afghan clothing, and his brother, wearing a Western suit. The first one hanging from a length of plastic tubing wrapped around his chest under his arms, the other strung up by the neck. Najibullah's face is recognizable, but blue, mottled with bruises: He must have been beaten before he was hanged. His brother's face, untouched, has a waxen pallor. The Taliban have stuffed cigarettes into the ex-president's mouth and crammed his pockets full of paper money, letting the bills stick out on purpose to advertise his greed. Najibullah seems to be vomiting cigarettes.

It's a vile spectacle, so ghastly that my sister and I start sobbing, but I can't tear my eyes away.

Papa parks the car some distance from the square, to avoid the crowd.

"I'm getting out, but you stay here. Whatever you do, stay in the car! I saw the pharmacist, he wound up coming here too, so I'm going to go speak with him."

Soraya and I are left alone, huddled against each other, watching the movements of the mob in the distance.

Farad was telling the truth: The Taliban are brandishing whips—or rather, some sort of wire cables—with which they lash out fiercely at passersby, forcing them to look at the grotesquely dangling bodies. I can't see these whips clearly; Soraya claims they have lead weights at the tips, but I'm not sure about that.

"But they do, look carefully! That one's beating a boy; you see how it's hurting him? A simple cable wouldn't make him suffer that much."

Ten minutes go by. Alone in the car, slumped in the

backseat, hiding under our chadors, we both sit in silence, thinking about the disaster that has befallen us and anxiously wondering what lies ahead. So many rumors are flying around. I won't be going to my classes anymore. And Mama? She studied at Zarghuna High School, where she didn't wear the veil; her father had bought her a bicycle, like mine, to ride to school. She knew a time when girls wore their skirts hemmed at the knee, like mine; she received her nurse's diploma, worked in a hospital, earned a degree in gynecology. Even today, at forty-eight, although she has retired, worn out from raising five children and working all her life to provide medical services for women, she still sees patients for free in her home two or three times a week.

Our country needs its women. For years, women have held jobs in the civil service, education, and health care. There are so many widows, so many children, so many preventive measures to be taken, so many medical emergencies to cope with, so many daily battles with people's ignorance of modern medicine. Mama has lived through difficult times, and the Taliban's entry into Kabul will weaken her even more.

In the distance, we see Papa coming back, his shoulders hunched; he opens the car door and slips behind the wheel, shaking his head without a word. We do not disturb his silence.

Then he starts the car, pulls away from the curb, and begins to speak.

"I talked with the pharmacist. His brother says that just before Massoud's troops left the city, someone close to the general went to the UN building to warn Najibullah and offer to take him along with them. Najibullah turned the man down. 'I'm writing my book,' he said, 'and the Taliban will give me another important position. Perhaps I'll be prime minister. I'm staying!' "

Many people did indeed think that if the Taliban seized power, the king really would return and Najibullah would rejoin the government. And now he's hanging in Aryana Square.

"He remained in the UN compound without any protection," continues Papa. "Around 4 A.M. the head of the Pakistani intelligence service arrived with an agreement—prepared in advance for Najibullah's immediate signature—that officially recognized the current Pakistani border, which includes the entire region of Peshawar that used to belong to our country. The man also wanted him to reveal the whereabouts of all the arms and munitions depots left behind in Kabul by the Soviets. Najibullah wouldn't sign. They beat and killed him, then strung him up on Aryana Square. It's his fault if he died like that. It's his fault. He didn't believe the Taliban would dare invade a building belonging to the United Nations. Well, they dared. God knows what else they're capable of after that."

We believe what Papa has told us, because he knows the pharmacist well, they often play chess together, and each considers the other a trustworthy friend. The man's brother left the city sometime this morning. He has no intention of handing over his weapons.

We return to our apartment, driving slowly to take in what's happening in the streets. Women carrying children or dragging them along by the hand walk quickly, heading home after going out in search of news. The city is so quiet that you can hear the patter of their footsteps. A few teenagers have gathered to discuss what they've seen at the square, talking with dramatic gestures, and Najibullah's name is on everyone's lips. We race up the stairs to avoid any questions from our neighbors.

Mama sighs with relief as we come through the door. Her prematurely gray hair is pulled back in a knot; her face is pale, and her dark eyes seem black with anguish.

"So? Did you see, is it really him?"

My father tells her about it, while I chime in. My mother suddenly feels faint and sits down. Soraya, who hasn't said much until now, starts talking about the Taliban's whips, but Papa gestures for her to be quiet. Mama cannot stand emotional shocks, and the doctor has advised us to try not to expose her to any stress.

Papa goes off to see our neighbor again but returns disappointed. The telephone still doesn't work, and neither does the radio. My father thinks about laying in a supply of batteries before this evening. The basic provisions—such as rice (the basis of our diet), pasta, oil, and flour (in case the bakeries shut down)—have already been taken care of. Papa saw to that at the beginning of the week, in preparation for what promised to be savage fighting.

There isn't any electricity, but we're used to that. In Kabul, electricity is a fickle sprite, arriving punctually for two or three days, then vanishing, leaving us to our gas or oil lamps. For cooking and hot water, we use a small gas cooker fueled by ten- or fourteen-liter bottles that are easy to find but impossibly expensive. We have a bathroom with faucets that ran dry a long time ago. All the plumbing is inoperative in our neighborhood as well as everywhere else. We press our clothes with an iron heated over a charcoal fire, and if the iron is still hot afterward, we offer it to a neighbor. We share and trade a lot in Kabul: Nothing useful should be wasted.

Finally, at 11 A.M., the radio station—rebaptized Radio Sharia—comes back on the air, with a long period of religious chanting, followed by a man's voice reciting a verse of the Koran. Then the Taliban decree:

"The Prophet told his disciples that their work was to forbid evil and promote virtue. We have come to restore order. Laws will be established by religious authorities. Previous governments did not respect religion. We have driven them out and they have fled. But all those who belonged to the former regime will now be safe with us. We ask our brothers to hand over their weapons, to leave them outside the front doors of their buildings or at a mosque. And for reasons of security, we ask that women stay in their homes during this first period of transition."

This speech, delivered in a harsh, singsong voice, is followed by religious chanting until noon. Then there is silence again. We'll have to wait until this evening, when we might be able to learn more from the Persian-language broadcast of the BBC or the Voice of America.

What can we do in the meantime, except assume the worst, going over and over the awful things we've seen? We even forget to eat lunch.

There's a knock at the door. It's the landlord's agent, following the Taliban's orders, coming to warn my father that he must take his weapons to the local mosque. We have no weapons, aside from two relics hanging on the wall. Papa looks at the old gun, an antique from the 1920s, a souvenir from his father's military service during the struggle against the British. After my grandfather died, Papa carefully hung his gun on our living room wall, and now it is just a decoration. A saber hangs beside it. What use would the Taliban have for such a weapon? Tears well up in my father's eyes, and I can see that he hesitates to part with these mementos. Mama insists, however, begging him to be reasonable.

"Hiding the gun would be too dangerous. They might search the house."

Then, with a heavy heart, Papa unhooks the old gun, which leaves a ghostly outline on the wall, just above a magnificent portrait of Mama painted by her brother. It's such a beautiful picture of her. She was twenty years old: Her glossy black hair falls in waves over her shoulders, and her large eyes sparkle with happiness. She is still beautiful, just a little worn by time and its trials.

Papa also unhooks the big saber, silently wrapping it up into a package with the gun. Later he will go off alone to leave his keepsakes at the mosque with the white flag.

I feel I'm going to cry. In our family, we try not to show our feelings when we're upset; we all keep our grief to ourselves. What's the use of inflicting on others a distress that will only make them feel even worse? It's a character trait that is typically Afghan—this emotional dignity and discretion on such occasions. We are quite talkative and outgoing about matters that don't hurt us inside, but we hardly ever speak about our sorrows. I think the civil war exacerbated this discretion, this reserve. We survive in a kind of economy of emotions that keeps us from collapsing, from going insane with rage and fear. When the pain is too great, when I feel it threatening to overflow in front of my family, I hide in my room to bury my face in my pillow and lie sobbing, alone on my bed.

On this Friday, the twenty-seventh of September, a day

fraught with visions of terror, Soraya and I talk endlessly about what has happened. After Shakila got married, I abandoned my single bed to sleep with Soraya. Until now, she used to talk to me about her trips, tell me stories about her colleagues on the flight crews. We'd listen to music, and she would make me laugh by jokingly pinching my nose to keep me from breathing. That was our way of dealing with the disturbing rumble of the explosions around the city. We practiced something our brother Wahid taught us that he learned when he was a soldier at the front: When there is a violent blast, you must open your mouth wide to prevent any injury to your eardrums.

Our bedroom is a refuge that reflects the passionate interests of my adolescence. On the wall is a poster of Brooke Shields, the American model who became an actress. Soraya has often entertained me by pretending to be a model: Teetering on her high heels, hands on her hips, wearing makeup, she would sashay around our room, posing and pirouetting. Even when I was little, she would dress up for me in our mother's clothes and shoes.

Next to the poster of Brooke Shields is one of Elvis Presley. My favorite music is rock, and I have heaps of audio cassettes. I also have lots of Indian movie videos that Daoud gets downtown from Farad's father, who runs a store that we love.

But today I don't feel like listening to music, I

couldn't possibly read; I just need to talk. Soraya is more devastated than I am, more dispirited. Her flight attendant's uniform is hanging in the closet, and there it will stay: She's convinced she will never wear it again. It looks so nice on her! Two days ago, she came home from the Bagram Airport in the long white blouse and turquoise pants of the Aryana Airlines uniform. Soraya takes after my father, and I think she's quite beautiful with her raven black hair down to her shoulders, her lovely eyes, and dark, velvety eyebrows. Like Shakila, she has always spoiled me. Ever since I was a baby, she has taken special care of me, and when I sometimes don't feel like doing my household chores, she does them for me. Soraya is sweet, plump, and affectionate, and she loves good food. This evening, however, she hasn't swallowed even a mouthful of rice.

Over and over again, we review everything we know from the massacres in the city of Herat in the spring of 1995, to what we've heard on the BBC about the Taliban's advance to the gates of Kabul. On television we saw widows, enveloped head to toe in their *chadris,* beaten with whips and forced to beg in the streets. Today such things are no longer distant images, news flashes on a TV screen: They are here, and they are only too real. Yesterday afternoon was perhaps my last outing in freedom, my last day as a student.

Now, I explain to Soraya why I felt such a need to go to Aryana Square.

"I wanted to see Najibullah, I was even ready to be flogged, to suffer, if necessary, in order to accept reality, to make some sense out of it. Do you see what I mean, Soraya? I wanted to convince myself. . . ."

My sister understands. "That image of those men, hanging there—I can't get it out of my head, Latifa, along with the idea that it's all over, that the Taliban are worse than anything I could imagine. Those corpses are a symbol they shoved in our faces to show us that from now on, anyone at all can die at the hand of a *talib*. Everything is finished for us. My career is gone. I'll never fly again. Did you see the Aryana Airlines building? They closed it, and the TV building too. No woman will be able to work anymore."

"Papa told us that in a few days, a few weeks, it might all have ended. The resistance is somewhere in the north—the mujahideen will come back, and I personally prefer the rockets to the Taliban."

"Papa always tries to give us hope, but I don't believe it. Even during the worst battles, we never saw such things. If you want proof, in 1992, when the mujahideen captured Kabul, no one hanged Najibullah! Or his brother, even though that guy was a miserable creep."

When she was still working as a journalist in Kabul, Shakila had told us the sordid story of Najibullah's brother, Shapour, who had an affair with a young girl. Many people in Mikrorayan had suspected as much. The girl's name was Wida, and she lived in one of the housing complexes. She had met Shapour on the main square, and from then on he would see her after classes at her high school. One day he accompanied her home when the rest of her family was out. I don't know who dragged whom into the empty apartment, but everyone has a pretty good idea who was responsible for what happened. Unfortunately, Wida became pregnant, so her lover had to be persuaded to marry her. In spite of her pleading, he wouldn't agree to a wedding, so Wida invited him to her home for one last discussion. When he still refused to marry her, she grabbed his revolver and killed herself. At first no one dared say anything, but then serious rumors began circulating, blaming Shapour for her death. Wida's parents quickly went into exile, because in those days Najibullah's brother was untouchable.

"Whatever his crimes were," says Soraya, "it's a barbaric way to die. His killers aren't Afghans, it's impossible. When I returned from Dubai Wednesday, I told you there were some Afghans on the plane that landed immediately after ours, and the flight attendant told me they had just been expelled from the Emirates because they had no passports, or their visas had expired, I don't remember now. Anyway, my friend was struck by their behavior: They were extremely rude to the women on the crew. I wonder whether they weren't coming in from abroad to help the Taliban."

You never know who's who in Kabul. The only safe rule is not to say what you really think except when you're with your own family. On principle, we stay as neutral as possible. One thing, and one thing only, unites Afghans in spite of their ethnic divisions: resistance against all foreign invaders, be they British, Pakistani, Arab—or Soviet, of course.

The Afghans revolted against the Russian occupation, organizing their resistance as best they could, and to drive out the Soviet army, the mujahideen began a war that lasted through ten bloody years and a series of interchangeable governments that were all under the heel of Moscow.

After the Russians left, the former resistance fighters set themselves up in Kabul in 1992 under the leadership of General Massoud. For years we endured the fighting that pitted him—a Tajik—against the other warlords, beginning with his Pashtun enemy, the ferocious Gulbuddin Hekmatyar, the head of the most fundamentalist faction, the Hizb-i-Islami, which was supported by Pakistan. But that wasn't the end of the story. We have just been forced into a new era, under the lash of the Taliban. Today is the most dreadful day of my whole young life.

Soraya is crying. She has never experienced the war in this way. The last time Hekmatyar pounded the city with rockets, on January 1, 1994, she was en route to Dubai. The airport in Kabul had already been destroyed, so Aryana's planes were using the airfield in Bagram, twenty-five miles north of the capital. Landing in the middle of the fighting was unthinkable, so the pilot flew on to New Delhi, where Soraya was marooned for six months, miserably watching television all day long in the hotel with her colleagues. Two years ago, on Shakila's wedding day, more than three hundred rockets fell on the city while we were busy celebrating. I remember the proverb our family kept reciting to reassure ourselves: "Joy and sorrow are sisters."

Shortly after Shakila's marriage, Wahid left for India, before going to live in Moscow. While he was still at home I felt both a deep love for my brother and a fear that was difficult to describe. Very strict about religious observances, he was the one who first gave us the chadors we are wearing today.

"Do you remember, Soraya? The day Wahid brought us these chadors? They were much too big for us."

"I told him we were going to cut them in half."

Our father did not agree with our eldest brother's insistence on dictating what we wore. Papa didn't want us to be different from the other students at school. In our home, the chador is reserved for prayers made in the privacy of one's room. We didn't wear it in the street, and neither did Mama. But I was ready to obey my brother, because I loved him. He would lecture us about the length of our skirts or the (modest) necklines of our T-shirts in the summer. Shakila and Soraya just let him talk; at the very worst they'd shoot back, "We're old enough to know what to wear, thank you," or "Mind your own business."

I think my parents feared the influence of fundamentalism on Wahid's character, and they advised him, after his military service and all the combat he'd seen, to go live in a country at peace. I wonder what he is doing now, and if he will get married one day. Many eligible young women were recommended to him, but he rejected them all. The army is not compatible with married life. Mama would rather that he live far away, that he no longer be involved in these battles that have already hurt him so deeply, and hardened him so terribly.

Daoud is pacing back and forth in his room. He escaped going into the army, protected as he was by all of us and by an older brother who felt that "one in the family is enough." Will he now have to disguise his identity again to be able to go on working? After his studies in economics, all he could find was a job at the ticket counter of Aryana Afghan Airlines.

They say the Taliban force young Afghan men in the provinces to join their army, sending them to the front lines to destroy villages, burn houses.

Daoud decides to go out instead of my father this

afternoon to buy some batteries in case the city is besieged. He's not the only one laying in supplies. Returning that evening, he tells us he saw lots of people on the same errand. Mama didn't want him to leave the apartment, and I hear her arguing with her son about the risk he took.

"What if they arrest you? What if they put you in prison, like the Communists did with your brother? Or what if they compel you to kill others?"

My poor father has the entire weight of the household on his shoulders. He's worried about Mama's health, he's afraid the Taliban will take his son, and he fears his daughters will be condemned to live shut up in their home, with no hope of a career. And he has no idea what state his textile warehouses are in—from what he can gather, they lay right in the path of the Taliban as they entered the city. The first time disaster struck was in 1991, during the failed coup d'état led by General Tanai, when rockets destroyed Papa's store on a major avenue, Jade Maywan. The whole shop went up in smoke. That store was very successful: Papa was earning a good living importing fabrics from Japan and the U.S.S.R., and although we weren't rich, we weren't poor, either. That day he lost a considerable part of his assets.

After many difficulties, he managed to reestablish his import business, but a second calamity occurred in 1993, while Hekmatyar was attacking Kabul. My father could not even get near his warehouse on Pole Mahmoud Khan, right in a combat zone riddled with antipersonnel mines. We saw smoking ruins on TV. Finally, three months later, Papa was able to go see for himself. There was nothing left to salvage in the debris scarred by bullets and explosives. Papa went to visit a hospitalized watchman who had survived and who told him about the hell he'd been through. When the wretched man had tried to persuade the attackers not to burn the warehouse with their flamethrowers, they shot him. They even shot the dogs! Seriously wounded, the watchman had played dead until a tank manned by government soldiers picked him up at the end of the day. Why would anyone burn warehouses, shoot civilians and even dogs? It was the bloodthirsty troops of Hekmatyar, desperately determined to defeat his enemy Massoud and retake Kabul. Once again my father had to start from nothing, helped by government loans to merchants who had suffered losses. He was able to revive his business and even to repay much of his loan. He thought he had put his troubles behind him, but after yesterday's fighting, we can't be sure of anything, and if he has a third catastrophe, I don't know how he could get back on his feet financially.

Finally, we listen to the BBC this evening, ears glued to the radio so that the neighbors can't hear us. The newscaster has nothing to report that we haven't heard before. He speaks of fighting between the government forces of

General Massoud and the Taliban on the outskirts of Kabul. Well, we already know that the battle is no longer "on the outskirts" but in the capital itself, in our very lives.

And that tonight we must try to sleep in the midst of this nightmare.

TWO

A Canary in a Cage

A postcard tacked up by Soraya on our bedroom wall shows a splendid purple rose on a blue background. I've been staring at it ever since my sister got up to prepare breakfast.

Dawn on this Saturday, the twenty-eighth of September, 1996, has the taste of ashes. Yesterday, the neighbors were talking worriedly in the hallway, trying to find out if the phones were working again, if any news had been heard from their respective families. Today, I hear only a heavy silence. My father won't go running this morning. The Taliban certainly don't approve of jogging, and Papa has other things to worry about. The banks were closed yesterday, as they are every Friday, but he must go this morning to withdraw money for the days to come.

Mama is still asleep, wiped out by sedatives. I don't hear any music in Daoud's room. He must be whispering in the kitchen with Soraya, trying not to wake our mother. They won't be going to work this morning, and I won't be going to my classes.

I am tired to the bone. I feel a sorrow that weighs down my whole body yet leaves me unable to weep. I just lie on my bed. Why get up? I gaze at my sister's collection of postcards on the wall. A red tulip, some sort of white flower from New Delhi . . . Soraya adds to her paper garden wherever she goes. There haven't been any flowers here in Kabul for a long time, aside from plastic bouquets imported from Taiwan.

What is there to do? I've already said my prayers on the rug Papa brought me from Mecca. I could read the latest article my friend Saber sent me for the little review we put out. A bunch of us have been collaborating on this project—entitled *Fager,* which means *Dawn*—for about two years now, producing a single copy of each issue, which passes around the neighborhood from hand to hand before returning to me in a rather dilapidated condition. Our most recent effort is filed away on one of my shelves, and we're working on the next issue. But now, what's the use of collecting photos and writing articles about Madonna, poetry, the latest fashion, or a new Indian film? If the Taliban control the media, there won't be anything for us to glean from the press, which will be censored or even cease to exist at all.

Last Thursday morning I passed the first part of the entrance exam for the journalism department at the university with flying colors. That same evening, Saber and his sister Farida asked me if I were really studying hard enough for the second part, scheduled for the beginning of winter.

I shrugged off their misgivings.

"Today was easy!"

"But what was the subject?"

"Each student had to choose a topic and develop it for three different media: radio, television, and the press."

"What news item did you pick?"

"A real one, in theory, although no one knows what the actual source was: Osama bin Laden, a Saudi friend of the Taliban, has offered to finance the construction of mosques in Afghanistan."

I had heard that on the radio, I don't remember when anymore, but it had made an impression on me. I knew almost nothing about this bin Laden, however, except that as a Saudi he had to have a lot of money. I received a good grade on my exam.

Before leaving, Saber returned a book he had borrowed from me: *A Red Flower for My Sorrow*, by the Iranian writer Parwiz Ghasi Saïd. A sad love story that all the kids my age are trying to get their hands on at the moment and that I just loved.

"Well, what did you think of it?"

He makes a face, so as not to seem sentimental, although he's in love with a girl from the neighborhood. He tells me everything, and I repeat it all to his sister. I also know that his parents think Saber is much too young to begin engagement negotiations with the girl's family.

I try to think about cheerful, frivolous things, like my dress that Papa promised me he'd pick up from the seamstress. Mama gave him a reproachful look—she thinks he lets me get away with too much. I adore my father, and I can wheedle just about everything I want from him. When Daoud was a student, even he came to me if he needed something from Papa. Whenever I ask for money to buy a tape or some nail polish, Mama lectures me.

"Don't be silly, Latifa! We have to stick to our family budget!"

Yesterday, she was sincerely shocked that I could still think about the wedding at a time like that. But I hadn't even gotten to see the finished dress yet. . . .

Maybe I'm revealing a shallow side to my character, but I need to cling to the "normality" of my life as an ordinary girl. It's a way of denying the imprisonment that is lying in wait for me, lying in wait for every Afghan girl and woman. It's inevitable.

I can always just stay here staring at that cardboard

rose. It's like an obsession, like an iron band around my forehead: I won't be going to classes anymore; I passed that exam for nothing; I'll remain shut up inside our apartment, without any goal or plan for the future. For how long? Weeks, months will go by before the resistance can chase away these white carrion crows. Years, perhaps. No one knows where General Massoud and his men have gone. "They have been driven out," announced Radio Sharia, and it will be a long time before we learn anything more.

Breakfast is a dreary affair; Radio Sharia isn't at all like Radio Kabul. It doesn't have a news program anymore; the broadcast will begin at eleven o'clock, as it did yesterday, with religious chants and decrees by the mullahs.

I hate this empty, meaningless morning. Before, it was a pleasure to breakfast on warm bread and sweet tea while listening to the program *Payam Sobhgahan* on Radio Kabul: the daily news, Persian poetry, music. Around eight o'clock, Daoud and Soraya would leave for work and I'd go off to my classes. Only Mama would stay home, with Bingo for company. On certain days she would give free consultations to neighborhood women whose husbands were very strict and refused to let them be taken care of by male doctors at the hospital. For precisely this reason, most of the doctors in Kabul are women, especially the gynecologists.

Waiting for Radio Sharia to deign to inform us of the

new regime's orders, we're allowed to hear nothing from eight to nine except religious chanting, a reading of verses from the Koran, and prayers. Daoud will turn on the radio periodically, in the unlikely event that there's something worth hearing.

I go back to my room to lie down while Soraya washes the dishes. Papa will attempt a cautious foray into the neighborhood to do some shopping, go to the bank, and try to pick up scraps of information in the homes of trusted friends. Mama stretches out on the living room sofa and is soon dozing. The life has gone out of her eyes. She didn't even scold me when she saw Soraya doing the dishes for me. She seems to have no interest in anything this morning.

When Papa returns, he brings bad news. The banks are still closed, stores and offices as well. Only the Ministries of Defense and the Interior are functioning. Papa has seen shattered TV sets lying all over like garbage and tangles of cassette tape hanging in trees, swaying in the autumn breeze like sinister wreaths. The streets are full of gloomy people, and there are long lines in front of the few stores that are open.

My father is going to the mosque now to hand over the family's antique arsenal, wrapped in a rag. My poor Papa, so sturdy, so resilient, so respectable—what a humiliation! He hasn't shaved this morning; his face is gray, sad, and the stubble on his cheeks makes him look ill.

Eleven o'clock. Radio Sharia comes back on to announce that the prime minister of the interim government, which is composed of six mullahs, has issued the following statement.

"From now on the country will be ruled by a completely Islamic system. All foreign ambassadors are relieved of their duties. The new decrees in accordance with Sharia are as follows.

"Anyone in possession of a weapon must hand it in to the nearest mosque or military checkpoint.

"Women and girls are not permitted to work outside the home.

"All women who are obliged to leave their homes must be accompanied by a *mahram*: their father, brother, or husband.

"Public transportation will provide buses reserved for men and buses reserved for women.

"Men must let their beards grow and trim their mustaches according to Sharia.

"Men must wear a white cap or turban on their heads.

"The wearing of suit and tie is forbidden. The wearing of traditional Afghan clothing is compulsory.

"Women and girls will wear the *chadri*.

"Women and girls are forbidden to wear brightly colored clothes beneath the *chadri*.

"It is forbidden to wear nail polish or lipstick or makeup.

"All Muslims must offer ritual prayers at the appointed times wherever they may be."

As the days go by, decrees rain down on us at the same hour from Radio Sharia, chanted with the same threatening voice in the name of Islamic law.

"It is forbidden to display photographs of animals and human beings.

"A woman is not allowed to take a taxi unless accompanied by a *mahram*.

"No male physician may touch the body of a woman under the pretext of a medical examination.

"A woman is not allowed to go to a tailor for men.

"A girl is not allowed to converse with a young man. Infraction of this law will lead to the immediate marriage of the offenders.

"Muslim families are not allowed to listen to music, even during a wedding.

"Families are not allowed to photograph or videotape anything, even during a wedding.

"Women engaged to be married may not go to beauty salons, even in preparation for their weddings.

"Muslim families may not give non-Islamic names to their children.

"All non-Muslims, Hindus, and Jews must wear yellow clothing or a piece of yellow cloth. They must mark their homes with a yellow flag so that they may be recognizable.

"All merchants are forbidden to sell alcoholic beverages.

"Merchants are forbidden to sell female undergarments.

"When the police punish an offender, no one is allowed to ask a question or complain.

"All those who break the laws of Sharia will be punished in the public square."

This time, they're really killing us, killing all girls and women. They're killing us stealthily, in silence. The worst prohibitions, which have already been established throughout the great majority of the country, annihilate us by locking us outside of society. All women are affected, from the youngest to the oldest. Women may no longer work: This means a collapse of medical services and government administration. No more school for girls, no more health care for women, no more fresh air for us anywhere. Women, go home! Or disappear under the *chadri,* out of the sight of men. It's an absolute denial of individual liberty, a real sexual racism.

As a last insult to all Afghans, men and women, a new minister has been appointed. He bears the ridiculous title of Minister for the Promotion of Virtue and Prevention of Vice, or *AMR Bel Mahrouf* in Afghan.

I go to my room to look at all my things: my books, clothes, photos, comics, music tapes, videos, and posters. My nail polish, Soraya's lipstick . . . We'll have to pack all this up in cardboard boxes and hide it in the closet. I'm crushed, at moments enraged, in tears a second later. My mother and sister and I find this petty tyranny over our personal lives intolerable. Mama has begun to wrap up forbidden items, family albums, baby pictures, photos of weddings—hers and Shakila's. Mama has taken down her lovely portrait painted by her brother, the picture of a woman in full bloom, an image of liberty the Taliban cannot stand. While Soraya and I pile our girlish treasures into the closet, our mother hides her own keepsakes from her years as a student, young woman, wife, and mother, concealing them in the back of a kitchen cupboard. I pack my prettiest dresses into a suitcase, keeping only pants and black running shoes. Soraya does the same thing. Her pretty Aryana Airlines uniform, her short, colorful skirts, her spring blouses, her high heels and rainbow-hued sweaters, now "indecent." Then Soraya helps Mama go through the apartment to hunt down forbidden pictures, including calendars and the football and music posters in Daoud's room.

And I break down and cry, alone in the middle of our bedroom with the last books to be packed away. I feel faint. While I was busily filling boxes, I was acting as if I were just temporarily putting my things into storage. Now I feel as though I were coming apart. I happen to notice a cartoon I cut out of a newspaper last year. It shows two scientists bending over a microscope, studying some *talibs* swarming on a specimen slide. The scientists seem perplexed and wonder what kind of germ they're looking at.

A nasty germ, a dangerously virulent microbe that propagates by spreading a serious disease insidiously fatal to the freedom of women. This microbe is highly infectious. The Taliban need only declare themselves through force the absolute masters of Sharia, the precepts of the Koran, which they distort as they please without any respect for the holy book. In my family we are deeply religious; my parents know what the Sharia means for a good Muslim. And the injunctions of the Koran have nothing to do with what the Taliban want to impose on us.

The Taliban have already forbidden us to keep photos of animals; soon they will forbid us to keep the animals themselves, I'm sure of it. We have a canary in a cage on the living room balcony, which Papa converted into a glassed-in porch to protect us from the cold and from prying eyes. Our bird sings so sweetly at sunrise.

Returning from the mosque, Papa finds me sobbing in my room.

"Calm down, Latifa! Nobody knows yet how things

will turn out. You must be patient. This won't last, you'll see."

"Papa, we have to let the canary go. I want him, at least, to be free!"

Opening this cage is a vital symbolic gesture. I watch the canary hesitate before this unfamiliar freedom, take flight in a flurry of wings, and disappear into the distance in the cloudy September sky. It's my liberty he carries away with him. May God guide him safely to some peaceful valley!

Everything has changed; the world is upside down. My father still rises early for his morning prayers, but can no longer go jogging because the Taliban will not allow anyone besides themselves to run in the street. Soraya, Daoud, and I get up at around nine or ten o'clock, without any energy, without any enthusiasm. My father and brother are obliged to grow beards, and we all feel our faces drooping from sadness and fatigue. No one turns on the radio now because there is no more news, no more music, no more poetry. Nothing but propaganda.

And decrees:

"It is forbidden to whistle and to own whistling teakettles.

"It is forbidden to keep dogs or birds."

I was right. Luckily, our canary is already long gone.

We, and no one else, granted him his liberty. But now we must part with Bingo, our white greyhound, whose fur is so dense he looks like a bear cub. He has always been part of my life. My first memory of him goes back to a color photograph in the album Mama hid in the kitchen. I'm about five years old, wearing a kilt, a red polo shirt, and a straw hat. I'm hugging Bingo, who is standing on his hind legs with his long muzzle pointing toward my oldest sister, Shakila, as if to say, "Rescue me! I was made to run around on all four legs!"

There's no question of us setting him loose in the streets, as some dog owners have done with their pets. So Papa drives Bingo to my uncle's house, which has a garden. Bingo, the four-legged Afghan dissident, will be hidden inside the house during the day and go out for some fresh air in the evening. I know they will take good care of him.

Our father has lost his business once again. He wasn't able to go check on his warehouse until three weeks after the arrival of the Taliban. Keeping a good distance away because of the mines hidden all around, he could see that his livelihood had been reduced to ruins. He doesn't complain, so as not to burden Mama with fresh worries. He'll make arrangements with an associate in Pakistan, investing the funds he has left in some new enterprise in the hope of earning a decent revenue. But it will be a difficult endeavor; he won't be able to go to work every day, and he will miss that. From now on he, too, will be something of a prisoner in our apartment, in charge of the shopping and cooking, which won't bother him in the least. He has always cooked, especially when Mama was working at the hospital.

His beard has grown long enough for us to tease him occasionally about this new face of his, or about whether his beard is long enough to suit the Taliban. He reacts with a mixture of composure and cool contempt.

"My beard belongs to the Taliban, but I don't!"

Daoud and some of his buddies have already found a way to scrounge videos on the sly; they're smuggled in from Pakistan through channels that have been around for ages. Besides, my uncle still has some in his store. Which, by the way, is a rather curious paradox: We're not allowed to buy VCRs, TVs, or video and audio cassettes, yet these items are always available in the stores. Nobody buys them officially; everybody obtains them unofficially. It seems the Taliban hypocritically turn a blind eye, unwilling to destroy a black market that would wipe out all of Kabul's commerce if it collapsed.

Life at home is punctuated by the comings and goings of Papa and Daoud. They are the ones who bring news from the outside world, from the bazaar, the vegetable seller, the business district, or the mosque. And we listen to them greedily.

"Afghans are disgusted by the way the Taliban distort our religion with their laws. We have always been Muslims, and no one sees anything familiar in their brand of Islam. They make people stop anywhere in the street to pray. One man said he'd been stopped five times in a row and had to pray each time! They also say that at the mosque, when the moment arrives to ask God for our dearest wish, many men beg, 'My God, get rid of these Taliban!' They can force us to pray all they want, but we can still pray for what *we* want."

The days are endless tunnels of inactivity. I spend most of my time lying down in my room, staring at the ceiling or reading. No more jogging in the morning, no more bike riding—I'm slowly going to seed. No more English classes, or newspapers; I stupefy myself with the simpering sentimentality of the Indian films Daoud brings home. So that the Taliban won't see the glow of the TV screen after curfew, my uncle came over to paint the windows of our bedrooms, the living-room porch, and the dining and family rooms, which overlook the street. Now only the kitchen window affords a glimpse of the mosque and the school, where there's nothing to see anymore but a circle of boys around the mullah, reciting the Koran.

I can't think of anything to do. Sometimes I wander

around my home like a convict taking a tour of her cell. I go sit in an armchair, then on a couch or on the rug. I stroll down the hall to the kitchen, then back to my room. Sit down, stretch out, study the designs on the carpets for a while, try the TV again, go lie down once more. I have never before paid such close attention to the furnishings of the apartment. A breadcrumb on the table attracts my notice. A bird in the sky fascinates me. Without realizing it, I'm already becoming depressed, deprived of all focus. Mama is far away, dozing, and no longer takes any real interest in what Soraya and I are doing, since we're not doing anything.

Saber visits me occasionally. Sometimes Mama sees patients, who arrive in their *chadris*. They're from the neighborhood, always uneasy, always in a hurry. I let them in; they disappear into the living room with Mama. Their husbands wait for them downstairs.

One day, at the end of the winter, I open the door to a woman in a *chadri*, thinking she's another patient who has come for a secret consultation. But the woman begins to ask me strange questions.

"You really are Latifa? Alia's daughter? Saber's friend?"

Put off by her behavior, I'm about to shut the door in her face when she insists on coming into the apartment.

"Yes, yes—it really is you!"

Suddenly she bursts out laughing, raises her *chadri*, and I recognize Saber's sister.

"Farida! It's you? You almost frightened me! Whatever are you going around in that thing for?"

"My older sister is here visiting us: I certainly fooled her! And now I've pulled the same trick on you! Not only that—I'm going to go out in it. Here, try it on."

It's a shock to see her dressed like that. I know what a *chadri* is; I'd seen them long before the Taliban came. Some women from the villages used to wear these traditional garments—of their own free will—when they came to consult Mama. In Kabul itself, however, one rarely saw them. On the other hand, during the civil war, the *chadri* could be quite useful to men and women passing along information. These anonymous feminine silhouettes with hidden faces sometimes concealed resistance fighters in pants. When we encountered such figures in the street, my friends and I would giggle at them. We called them "bottles" or "upside-down cauliflowers" or "grocery bags." When there were several of them, they were "paratroops."

I look at this *chadri*, a shapeless cloth tent sewn to a tight-fitting cap and covering the entire body. Some *chadris* are much shorter, certainly less inconvenient. The small embroidered openwork peephole covering the eyes and nose frightens me.

"My father bought us some. They're not as long as yours."

"My sister found this one at an aunt's house," explains Farida. "It's old, and my aunt was tall. Try it on. If you ever want to go outside, you'll have to wear one."

I put it on to humor her but also to find out what it feels like inside one of these things. The cloth sticks to my nose, it's hard to keep the embroidered peephole in front of my eyes, and I can't breathe.

"Well? Can you see me?" asks Farida.

I can see her—if I stay right in front of her. To turn your head, you have to hold the cloth tightly under your chin to keep it in place. To look behind you, you have to turn completely around. I'm hot, and I can feel my breath inside the tent. I'm tripping over the hem. I'll never be able to wear such a garment. Now I know why the "bottle-women" walk so stiffly, staring straight ahead or bending awkwardly over unexpected obstacles. I understand why they hesitate before crossing a road, why they go upstairs so slowly. These phantoms now condemned to wander through the streets of Kabul must have a hard time avoiding bicycles, buses, carts. And a hard time escaping from the Taliban. This isn't clothing, it's a jail cell.

If I want to go outside, however, I'll have to give in and wear one. Unless I disguise myself as a boy, cut my hair, or try to grow a beard, I have no other choice. At the moment, there's no way I can bring myself to hide beneath that thing. That tiny barred window grid looks like a canary cage. And I'd be the canary.

I come out from under there angry and humiliated. My face belongs to me. And the Koran says that a woman may be veiled, but should remain recognizable. The Taliban are trying to steal my face from me, to steal the faces of all women. It's outrageous! I'm not going out with Farida.

"You can't spend the rest of your life shut up at home!"

"All right, I'm scared. Scared of stumbling in it, of drawing attention to myself, of being beaten in the street because I let something show or I lifted this thing up to sneeze. . . . If I had to run to save myself, I'd never manage it."

"This one's too long, wear yours."

"No. I've heard they're kidnapping girls to marry them by force to Taliban soldiers."

"Well, I can't stay cooped up. My brother's going with me; you don't risk anything if you're with your brother. Ask Daoud to come along!"

"Absolutely not, I'm not going out. Anyway, I've no desire to see long lines of women scuttling through the streets. I'd be too depressed when I got home, if I did get home. . . ."

The programs on Radio Sharia are always the same: from 8 to 9 A.M., prayers and readings from the Koran; from 9 to 10:30, religious songs, propaganda, and the announcement of new decrees, some of which are chanted in Arabic, as if to make us believe they're really from the Koran. Then they suspend broadcasting until 6 P.M., when they read the "death notices" for Taliban "heroes." Then comes the "news," which is always the same, hailing Taliban advances without mentioning (of course) any conflicts with the resistance or any villages that are fighting off Taliban attacks. Finally, at 9:30 P.M., after the reading of a few sacred texts, Radio Sharia shuts up.

Around noon, one of us suggests halfheartedly that we fix something to eat. Our home is like a hospital or a penitentiary. The silence is oppressive. No one is doing anything anymore, so we have nothing to talk about. Since we can't talk to one another, we're left alone with our fear and dismay. And when everyone is in the same black hole, it's useless to keep saying we can't see any daylight.

I drag around, don't change my clothes anymore, sometimes wearing the same outfit for three or four days, day and night. The neighbor's telephone never rings anymore; it's still out of order. And when it finally does work again, my father hesitates to use it: We're well aware that the Taliban listen to everything, spy on everything.

Some of Daoud's friends come by the apartment now and then to watch videos in secret.

Farida and Saber occasionally drop in to visit me. They go out, they're more adventurous than I am, but I just don't dare risk setting foot outside. I feel as though the only way I can still resist is to shut myself in, refusing to see *them*.

It isn't until the very beginning of 1997, four months after the Taliban takeover, that Farida persuades me to venture into the streets of Kabul with her, under the pretext of retrieving the latest issue of our review from our friend Maryam, who recently borrowed it from me. I don't see why I have to go along on this errand.

"You must come outside!" insists Farida. "You look awful, and there's no better way to confront reality. If you stay shut in any longer, you'll go crazy."

I vanish under my *chadri*. Then Saber, Farida, and I begin our strange "walk." I haven't been outdoors for months. Everything seems strange to me, and I feel lost, as if I were a convalescent still too weak to be up and about. The street looks too big. I feel as though I were constantly being watched. We whisper under our *chadris* to avoid attracting attention, and Saber sticks close to our sides.

On the way to Maryam's we pass our former high school, there are Taliban guards at the entrance. On the adjacent sports field, ominous garlands of cassette tape have been draped on the volleyball net, the basketball hoop, and the branches of trees. My father had already mentioned them, but I'd thought these displays were temporary. Apparently, they are systematically renewed, streamers of forbidden pleasures: no images, no music.

A bit farther on, we pass four women. Suddenly a black 4×4 brakes to a halt next to them with a hellish screech: *Talibs* leap from the vehicle brandishing their cable whips and without a word of explanation begin flogging these women even though they're hidden by their *chadris.* They scream, but no one comes to their rescue. Then they try to run away, pursued by their tormentors, who keep whipping them savagely. I see blood dripping onto the women's shoes.

I'm frozen, I can't move, I've been turned to stone—and they're going to come after me next. Farida grabs my arms roughly.

"Run! We have to get away! Run!"

So with one hand I clamp the peephole of the chadri over my face, and we race off like lunatics until we're completely out of breath. Saber stays behind us, our helpless bodyguard—he knows there's nothing he could do to protect us. I have no idea if the *talibs* are following us; I seem to feel them breathing down my neck and keep expecting every second to feel their whips, to stagger beneath their blows.

Fortunately we're not far from home, so within five

minutes we're scrambling up the stairs of our building. On the landing I sob uncontrollably, gasping for air, unable to speak. Farida painfully catches her breath, muttering who knows what, probably cursing the Taliban. She's much more of a rebel than I am.

Saber has caught up with us. Horrified, he explains what happened.

"Farida, they beat those women for wearing white shoes."

"What? That's some new decree?"

"White is the color of the Taliban flag, so women are not allowed to wear white. White shoes mean they're trampling on the flag!"

Even though they seem to follow one another without rhyme or reason, these decrees have a certain logic: the extermination of the Afghan woman.

A woman went out one day covered only with a chador, holding the Koran clasped to her breast. The Taliban attacked her immediately with their whips.

"You have no right!" she protested. "Look at what is written in the Koran!"

During the struggle, though, the Koran fell from her arms, and none of her assailants made a move to pick it up. Now, the Koran must *never* be placed directly on the ground. If they really respected the Koran, the Taliban would know this. But they completely ignore the customary principles of our religion. Their decrees are just so many aberrations with regard to the sacred texts. The Koran specifically states that a woman may show her nakedness to a man if he is either her husband or her physician. To forbid women to consult a male doctor when women are at the same time forbidden to practice a profession—including that of medicine—is to attempt to destroy them. The paralyzing depression slowly overtaking our mother is an example of this torture, this negation of women.

My mother was a spirited, strong-willed woman who always felt free in her family, free in her studies, and free to choose a husband who had not been selected by her family. When she was in college, she wore skirts or pants. In the sixties, she used to go to the Zainab Cinema, and even took along her sisters. Women in Kabul were demanding their rights at that time, and during the Afghan Women's Year in 1975, the regime of President Daoud showed some democratic good sense when it decreed that "the Afghan woman has the same right as the Afghan man to exercise personal freedom, choose a career, and find a partner in marriage."

A feminist organization that tried to extend the application of this law into the most distant provinces of the country encountered enormous difficulties, running up against the traditional prejudices of the various tribes. Mama told me that in certain country villages, naughty children were threatened with "the woman without a veil," a real ogress. "She'll eat you up if you disobey me!"

Mama did her supervisory period as a nurse at Mastourat Hospital in Kabul, an institution reserved for women. She worked there with distinguished professors such as Dr. Fatahé Najm, Dr. Nour Ahmad Balaiz, and Dr. Kerramuddin. She belonged to the medical team that took care of the mother of King Mohammed Zahir Shah. During the Soviet period, she had a job at our neighborhood day care center, which allowed her to have me there while she was at work. One day when I was four, she rushed into the room in a fury, took me home in a taxi, and left again immediately. Years later, she explained to me that she had sharply rebuked the nurse in charge of vaccinating the children for using the same hypodermic needle for all of them, which risked spreading infection. This was in 1984, and my mother well knew the dangers of such a practice. She was summoned before the hospital administration that same day.

"You have no right to argue with a Soviet nurse."

"Even about a professional mistake? Do you know what she was doing?"

"The Soviets do as they please. You have no business interfering. You will apologize to this nurse, or I will be forced to consider you a counterrevolutionary."

"That woman committed a serious breach of medical protocol. She is a danger to the lives of Afghan children, and my pride as an Afghan woman will not allow me to apologize to her. I refuse."

"You are dismissed!"

Mama tried to recover her professional file from the health authorities, but oddly enough, it had disappeared. In an attempt to settle the matter, Minister Nabi Kamyar then offered her the chance to take a competitive examination in the medical specialty of her choice. She passed and was sent the following year to Prague for six months' training in gynecology. She earned the highest grade among the trainees. When she returned to Kabul, she went to see the minister.

"Thank you, and now I'm going to retire," she told him. "I will no longer work under Soviet supervision!"

He managed to persuade her to stay on with him at the Ministry of Health. She retired three years later, but continued to practice out of her home and fill in at the hospital from time to time, until the arrival of the Taliban.

My mother was not retreating to the apartment to cook and to raise her youngest daughter; she has never been a fanatical housewife, and my father was quite capable of dealing with things, even hiring a cook at one time so that Mama could devote herself to her profession. My mother is even more affected than her daughters by being unable to work. Soraya and I are young, there's no reason to lose hope, as Papa says. But he fears the worst for his wife, whom he sees forced more deeply into premature retirement with each passing day.

When Papa goes out, when friends visit us, the news is only of nightmarish, revolting, abominable scenes. How can anyone accept that a woman had her fingers chopped off in the middle of the street by the religious police because she was wearing nail polish? My father does his best to shield Mama from these reports of incredible violence.

But you don't even need to go outside to find yourself face to face with horror.

Early in the winter of 1997, we hear a woman wailing in the street.

"My son is innocent, he's innocent!"

Looking out the window, I recognize the mother of Aimal, a boy who lives in the building next door. Three *talibs* are beating her son with the butts of their Kalashnikovs. They strike methodically, especially on his ribs. Soraya and I move quickly back from the window to avoid being seen, but we can't escape the boy's pain. His shrieks are heart-rending.

Then, silence. The *talibs* have gone, leaving Aimal's mother sobbing over the motionless body of her son. When the doctors arrive to take him to the hospital, it's too late: Aimal has been dead for almost an hour.

Daoud finds out what has happened. Aimal had invited some pals over to watch a film on his VCR, in spite of the prohibition in effect. The *talibs* had burst into the apartment and caught the boys, aged fifteen to seventeen, red-handed. After breaking the television and the VCR and ripping out the cassette tape, the *talibs* ordered everyone outside. Then they demanded to know which boy owned these forbidden things, and Aimal stepped forward. As punishment, they made the boys slap one another, which is very humiliating for an Afghan, even for a boy. When Aimal didn't hit hard enough for their taste, a *talib* went over to him and said, "I'll show you how to do it."

And he attacked him first with his hands, then with his weapon. Aimal's mother tried to shield him with her body, but a *talib* slapped her and hurled her into some barbed wire. Then they all battered the boy with their rifle butts.

When the Taliban entered Kabul, Aimal's family was among those who waved scarves from their windows to celebrate the victory. Since she lost her son, Aimal's mother has been endlessly begging pardon of everyone for having welcomed the Taliban. She has gone out of her mind: She could never have imagined that they could murder her son, in cold blood, before her very eyes. Now she gathers stones to hurl at their cars when they drive by. They have caught and whipped her more than once, but she always does it again. She doesn't care if they flog her—what has she got left to lose?

In February 1997, I venture outside for the second time. Although they have forbidden women to work, the Taliban have promised to pay them their salaries for a few more months. Daoud and I accompany Soraya to the offices of Aryana Airlines, which are about a mile from our apartment. Since it's quite cold out, my sister and I are wearing long black dresses over dark sweaters and jogging pants. Our socks and running shoes are black, and our brown *chadris* are firmly anchored on our heads, so in theory there's no reason for the Taliban to be suspicious of us. The avenue has greatly changed since I last saw it. The television and airline company buildings are still closed and gloomy. Corrugated tin shacks have been set up a few yards from the entrances to the buildings, simple bins with doors cut out of them, doors reserved for women. That's where the *chadris* line up, going one at a time to have documents verified and to receive the appropriate compensation. I notice a small opening on one side, a sort of spy hole, and while we're waiting, I realize what it's for. A woman enters the container through the large opening and stands in front of the Judas hole, through which she hands her papers to a *talib* on the other side, who checks them and returns them to her along with a stack of afghanis.

The *chadri* isn't enough: They also have to have this shield of sheet metal between them and a woman. Just what is it they are afraid of? We are impure—but that doesn't stop them from slapping a woman with their bare hands and shoving her into barbed wire!

The women who have come today to get the money owed them begin to protest. Why are they being humiliated, refused entry into the building? Why are they being relegated to a tin shack?

One of the armed *talibs* sitting on the ground by the entrance to the container stands up to shoot a few rounds into the air and scare us. As far as I'm concerned, he succeeds. But Narguesse, a colleague of Soraya's and one of her best friends, is so infuriated that she rips off her *chadri* and screams, "It's disgraceful to treat us like this!"

Utter astonishment. She has dared signal her rebellion by showing in broad daylight the pretty face of an out-of-work flight attendant.

Then the other women become caught up in her fervor: Shouting angrily, they close in on the *talib*, who is quickly joined by other men who push us roughly inside the shack and drag away Narguesse, who struggles like a demon.

Once inside, we take off our *chadris*, shouting, "We won't leave here until you bring her back!"

There are only about twenty of us. I don't know if Daoud saw the disturbance—I don't think so. He probably thought the paperwork would take a long time and strolled off down the avenue. Everyone is talking at once inside the shack: We're all afraid for Narguesse and wondering what punishment she's suffering. Our sole means of exerting pressure is to stay here, with our faces uncovered, so that they hesitate to throw us out. It doesn't give us much leverage.

At last Narguesse reappears, extremely agitated; she is wearing her *chadri* again, but refuses to say anything. The *talibs* scream at us to get out.

Eight of us head back to Mikrorayan. Along the way, Narguesse tells us what happened.

The *talibs* took her to the former personnel office on the ground floor of the building and made her put her *chadri* back on.

"Why did you remove your *chadri*? Why are you trying to defy and offend us?"

"Because you have no right to keep women from working. No right to receive us today like dogs in that shack. We helped make this company a success and we didn't wear *chadris* in the planes or in the offices!"

"You're nothing but a woman! You have no right to speak, no right to raise your voice. You have no right to take off your *chadri*. The days when you could travel and walk around without a *chadri* are over!"

Twice Narguesse tried to take off her *chadri* again, she tells us, and twice they stopped her.

"If you try that once more, we'll kill you."

Luckily for her, one of the *talibs* guarding the shack came to warn his superiors that we were refusing to leave until she returned. After hesitating a moment, they pushed her outside.

"Get out! And keep quiet!"

She escaped severe punishment, perhaps even death, for having rebelled like that, but why did they let her go? Because they were afraid of having to control a handful of women? True, there weren't a lot of them, either. . . . Perhaps they'd received instructions? We'll never know.

Narguesse is still upset, seething with anger. She has always been willful and independent.

"We have to fight back. Today we couldn't do much because there weren't enough of us. But if tomorrow there are thousands of us, then we'll be able to overthrow these Taliban!"

We agree with her, but how can we rebel? Where can we meet? We risk endangering our families. We have no weapons, no freedom of expression, no press, no television. To whom can we appeal? How can we obtain outside help when we have no voices, no faces? We're ghosts.

This has been our first protest demonstration since the Taliban took over five months ago. I'm afraid. I'm still shaking inside when Daoud catches up with our little group on the way back to Mikrorayan.

This evening, in the apartment with its painted-over windows, in the gloom of the kerosene lamp, Soraya and I finally have something to tell our mother. But Mama, who used to be so defiant, places her tired hands sadly on her daughters' heads and sighs, "I'm sure you were very brave."

And with a sharp pain in my heart, I realize that she doesn't ever want to hear about war or rebellion again. Every night she swallows her sleeping pills to take refuge in a dreamless sleep . . . where the Taliban can't touch her.

THREE

Three Girls

From now on, the kitchen window and the apartment door are my only contacts with the outside world. In the morning, I contemplate the mosque and my school in the distance. During the day, sometimes I open the door to welcome Mama's clandestine patients, who continue to slip through the streets in their *chadris*, coming to seek her help. When their visits are over, I close the door behind them and go back to my room to lie down and quietly play music or watch films I've already seen at least ten times.

I don't feel well. A strange, indescribable exhaustion pins me to the bed next to Soraya as the two of us talk endlessly about all the things we no longer do. Even Daoud's birthday, last October, came and went without any fanfare. The dress I was supposed to wear to the wedding we didn't attend is packed away in a box, unwearable under the Taliban.

We so loved parties, weddings, family reunions where we were free to laugh and dance. There were shopping trips to buy makeup, music tapes, books. I miss the discussions coming home after classes with my girlfriends—some of whom, bolder than I was, used to laugh loudly when we saw any boys, and passed whispered judgment on their looks and clothes. The parents of a few of these fifteen- or sixteen-year-old girls were beginning to think about future fiancés. I'm much more reserved on that subject. I've always thought that I wouldn't marry anyone until I was sure of his personality, his past, and his family. And sure of being able to love him. I am a believer, I say my prayers, and I respect the traditions of our society. If my future husband asked me to wear a scarf or the chador outside our home, I would certainly do so, but there my submissiveness would end, and my parents agree with me.

Of course I understand that a woman cannot live in our culture without the protection of a man, be he her father, brother, or husband, because she has no existence on her own in society. I don't refuse this protection—on the contrary—but I want my independence and my freedom of thought. Soraya is single, which is a requirement for her job as a flight attendant. She says she's like me, that she'll marry only a man she has chosen herself. Neither Mama nor Papa wants to impose anything whatsoever on us in such matters. In any case, marriage is far from our minds, and the terrible times we live in make meeting other people almost impossible.

We don't see the rest of our family anymore; we don't see anyone, really, aside from the neighbors now and then, and after that episode in front of the Aryana Airlines building, my sister and I do not go out at all.

I rage helplessly against these Taliban who keep us in prison, and I'm overwhelmed by the dreadful thought that if they remain in power for a long time, my life will be ruined—unless we flee the country to join the mass of exiles and refugees, a possibility my parents refuse even to consider, and I agree with them.

Our only consolation is that we are relatively well off, which protects us from the hardships afflicting so many women in the streets. We are fortunate: We have enough to eat. But as the years go by, my sister and I will grow old without work, without love, without children. Soraya is pessimistic, resigned to her sadness, while I'm trapped in morbid inertia by the inner rebellion that's eating away at me.

There's a knock on our door. I recognize the hurried, insistent rapping of someone who has come to consult Mama in secret. It means, "Open up, quickly! Let me in. I don't want anyone to see me."

To see her? Who would recognize a woman under a

chadri? But fear has become second nature to women now: It's always with us. The fear of meeting a neighbor, of having to answer a question. We're suspicious of everything. I open the door to a dark brown *chadri*, which the woman removes as soon as the door closes behind her.

Her face is puffy, with bleeding, grotesquely swollen lips. She doesn't need to say anything. I take her immediately to the living room, where my mother will examine her. To give her some privacy, I go to my room. But through the wall, I can hear her crying, and Mama calls me a few moments later.

"Bring me some boiling water and bandages, hurry!"

I fill a pot, prepare the bandages, stand impatiently watching the water begin to simmer. Another one. Another humiliated woman, beaten, God knows why.

I look on as Mama cleans the wounds covering the woman's torso and sutures them with a surgical needle. A clandestine doctor needs to know how to do almost everything in a world gone mad. This patient tells us she has been flogged because she dared go out in the street by herself.

"Why were you alone?" my mother asks.

"My father was killed during the fighting of the winter of 1994. I have no husband, no brother, no son. How can I help going out alone?"

"How did you manage today?"

"A cousin agreed to come with me to your apartment."

To buy food, she had no choice except to go out on her own. But the Taliban never try to understand, they just lash out with their whips. And that's not all: They have other methods of attack. I learned this early on.

At the end of October 1996, I open the door to a new atrocity, a fresh crime against women.

Through the BBC World Service, we've learned that the mujahideen of Ahmed Shah Massoud, in alliance with the resistance fighters of his former enemy, the Uzbek chief Abdul Rashid Dostum, have launched a counteroffensive to the north of Kabul. Radio Sharia doesn't mention this, naturally, because Radio Sharia prefers to glorify the successes of Taliban heroes while ignoring their defeats. If we are to believe the mullah in charge of "news" bulletins here in Kabul, the Taliban have victoriously captured all of Afghanistan more than twenty times over! Under General Massoud, however, the resistance still holds 25 percent of the country, which the Taliban are trying to take over. Fighting continues in the region of Kohestan, north of the capital.

A few days after we hear about this counteroffensive, four *chadris* turn up at our door at around nine in the evening. One of the women shows us her face: It's Nafissa, a former classmate of Soraya's. The three young girls with her are her cousins, but they refuse to remove their *chadris*. Nafissa explains briefly that they're from the Shamali Plain, in Kohestan.

My father is worried because they are alone.

"There's no one with you?"

"A taxi driver agreed to bring us here."

Mama escorts the three girls into the living room and shuts the door behind her, while my father goes quietly downstairs with Nafissa to thank the taxi driver.

I hear the three girls sobbing behind the closed door, and Mama pleading with them to calm down so that they don't alert the neighbors. Leaving them in the living room, she writes a short note and calls for Daoud.

"Take this to my friend Dr. Sima, at Mikrorayan 2, and hurry, Daoud—there's only an hour left until curfew."

After ten o'clock, moving around the city is forbidden, and all lights must be out in private homes. The apartment windows have been painted to prevent people from seeing inside, but as an extra precaution, so that Mama may safely examine her three young patients by auscultation, Soraya and I stretch pieces of dark material over the windows.

Then Mama asks us to spread a large plastic tarp on the floor so that she can operate. Since she can no longer obtain fresh supplies from the hospital, she has no more clean surgical needles, so we boil water to sterilize the old ones, which Mama then places in a small basin of alcohol. I still don't know what's wrong with the girls, who huddle on the floor, weeping silently beneath their *chadris*. One of them rocks slowly back and forth, clutching her belly. I will never forget their despair and suffering, because while we wait for Daoud to return, Mama tells us in the kitchen what happened to these children.

"They're about your age, Latifa, fifteen or sixteen . . . Some *talibs* captured them during their offensive on the Shamali Plain, a band of about fifteen men. They raped them. All fifteen men. It's revolting, but . . . that's not all, they . . ."

Mama hesitates, and we understand how hard it is for her to explain these atrocities to her own daughters. Soraya's eyes fill with tears; I stare at my mother, so shocked and apprehensive that I stifle a cry.

"What? What?"

"They mutilated their genitals, they tore them."

That's all she will say, and goes back to take care of the three young victims. She must now disinfect, anesthetize, and sew them up with the few materials at her disposal. I don't even dare ask her how the girls will bear the agony. I don't even dare imagine. I block out the image of a pack of fifteen animals ferociously raping three girls my age, virgins, my sisters.

Daoud returns just before the curfew with Dr. Sima, who is so incensed by what she finds that Mama must urge her to control herself.

"You have to help me finish here, so calm down, get hold of yourself. Did you bring what I asked for?"

"Yes. I brought everything I had."

From ten that evening until four the next morning, they work on the girls, sewing them back up again. In our room, Soraya and I can hear the feeble groans of the victims and the brief murmurs of our mother and Dr. Sima. It is impossible to think about anything else, and impossible to sleep.

Girls out in the countryside don't live the way we do. Mother discovered this for herself during the Soviet occupation, when she was sent to work in Khandar for six months. There she provided medical services and tried to improve sanitary conditions. She told me how hard it was to talk about birth control, gynecological problems, or even simple female anatomy. One woman of thirty-nine or forty came to see her complaining about nausea and hot flashes, convinced that she was pregnant when she was actually going through menopause. She had never known a woman who had lived long enough to experience the change of life, so she had no idea what it was.

What the future once held for Nafissa's country cousins was a marriage arranged by their families. This gang rape has destroyed that future. What neighbor of their village, what tribal cousin would ever ask for them in marriage now? And even if the rape remains a secret, they will be tormented by their devastating shame.

After a rape, an Afghan woman is forced to marry her rapist, according to the cruel tradition still practiced here today, or condemning her to exile or death. I am not a violent person, but tonight I have realized that if this ever happened to me, I would be capable of killing my attacker and then killing myself.

Their painful and painstaking work completed, Mama and Dr. Sima talk in the kitchen over a glass of hot tea, while the three girls finally get some sleep in the living room. Mama proposes that her colleague open a clandestine doctor's office.

"There are too many sick women in the neighborhood. They come to me even from far away, as you see, and I can't cope by myself. I have no drugs, and almost no supplies. You, on the other hand, have grown children living abroad whom you could ask to send us all the medicine we need. You're more organized than I am. And I'm worn out, simply exhausted."

In Kabul, the post office operates on the simplest level, and the least little package might attract notice. Everything passes through Peshawar, in Pakistan: The money and goods Afghans outside the country send home to their families and friends must come through Peshawar. Even messages and letters travel the same route. Plus you have to have trustworthy agents, with a reliable network—which Dr. Sima has. Ever since the arrival of the Taliban, each time Mama has appealed to

Dr. Sima for a specific drug in an emergency, her friend has obtained it for her.

Without any hesitation, Dr. Sima agrees to set up a clandestine medical office. Tonight she has seen for herself the urgent need for such a measure. And then there are the women who are simply ill and have nowhere to go, since only men can be doctors—who can treat only men!

So what will become the most important underground medical clinic in Kabul has just gotten under way.

Mother's three young patients leave later that morning, with Nafissa and the taxi driver. I wonder what will happen to these girls. We never saw them again.

The situation worsens with each passing day; society is falling apart all around us, while we watch helplessly. Papa tells us there are more and more beggars in the city, mostly widows or women prevented from working. My classmate Anita's mother, who was a teacher in my high school, now does washing in people's homes to earn a living. Other women bake bread or traditional pastries that their sons sell in the street. Some women do embroidery, or make necklaces.

Daoud has recently seen kids peddling single cigarettes and a few tablets of aspirin. He also says that some young people have decided to sell drugs to help their families survive. The most lucrative business is the drug traffic on the border with Pakistan, to which the Taliban turn a blind eye. But they're still busily cranking out decrees: Mullah Omar, their leader and mastermind, has decided that the spaces in the openwork mesh on the *chadri* that allow women to see where they're going are too big! From now on, the weave must be tighter, but the mullahs give no indication of what size the openings must be. Perhaps smaller than a fiftieth of an inch?

Faced with such lunacy, my sister and I lose all our self-confidence, asking each other over and over, "What can we do? I mean, what are we supposed to do? Just curl up and die?"

I have actually been ill for a while. This morning I've got a fever and feel dizzy; if I try to get up, I fall back heavily on my bed. Mama thinks I'm having sudden drops in my blood pressure, but she doesn't know what could be causing that. The worst thing is that she is even more ill than I am.

She's sinking ever deeper into depression. We do our best to take care of her, but we have nothing to give her except sleeping pills. My father, who loves her so much, tries never to leave her side for a second. To lose Mama would be terrifying. She has always managed everything in our home, has always been organized, efficient, with a forceful personality. Added to the misery of all that's happening in Kabul, the sadness of seeing her like this is a constant extra burden none of us can shake off.

The only time when Mama seems her old self again is when she can take care of others or give them medical advice. Sometimes, though, she wishes she weren't seeing these troubled, needy women: She has nothing left to treat them with.

She recently saw a woman suffering from a hemorrhagic condition she could have cured with an injection costing 1,200,000 afghanis, but the money proved impossible to find. Before the Taliban, Mama could easily obtain this kind of medication at the hospital where she still filled in from time to time. Now she can't even go there herself. Cut off from her profession, she would be simply thrown out of the building, and punished to boot. And this inability to practice medicine torments her constantly; she certainly broods over it day and night, to the point of having nightmares about it.

"That woman will have complications, it's inevitable," she told us after she had to send her away untreated. "She may well die from an infection, when it would be so simple to cure her! One injection, that's all it would take."

A doctor's conscience cannot be easily stilled. And we understand her dismay: That such a benign ailment should lead to a woman's death because of a Taliban decree is unspeakable.

Early in the summer of 1998, my poor father has two

sick women at home: his doctor-wife and the feverish daughter she is too unwell to treat. In any case, my mysterious ailment is not something she is equipped to handle.

Papa calls a friend who is a doctor, begging him to come help us. As a man, however, the doctor is forbidden to treat women and is understandably afraid. Nevertheless, he will come, on one condition: that Papa promises never to tell a soul. That's all the thanks he asks.

There is nothing he can do for Mama's depression. On the other hand, he suspects she has diabetes, which she has never had before. He takes blood from both Mama and me.

"I'll give these samples to the lab under the names of my own wife and daughter," he tells my father. "I can say right now, however, that these two women must go to a hospital in Pakistan as soon as possible. Latifa is depressed as well, but the main problem is that she has pleurisy. There is fluid in her lungs. Don't wait too long."

Well, I've been sick for about three months, with some periods of remission; my fever is a recent development. So we will be leaving for Peshawar, but organizing the trip takes time. We have to find a car and a reliable driver.

Finally, everything is ready. Papa packs Mama's suitcase, Soraya packs the other bags. Daoud is staying home, because people say the Taliban want to take over modern apartments like ours in the well-to-do neighborhood of Mikrorayan. We'll be staying with Shakila's parents-in-law for as long as the treatments last.

Ordinarily, going to Peshawar poses no special problems, aside from a particularly dangerous road and the fact that Afghans are officially forbidden to leave the country. Many Afghans regularly do just that, however, going once or twice a month to get provisions, and the customs officials look the other way. What people do is say they're going to Jalalabad, then negotiate passage through several heavily manned checkpoints on the way to the border, which Pakistan decided unilaterally to adjust in its own favor. My oldest brother often said that Pakistan has been dreaming of annexing our country for a long, long time.

This is our first trip since the Taliban seized power almost two years ago. Summer is here, it's hot, and the stifling *chadri* is of course de rigueur for Mama, Soraya, and me.

At dawn, the station wagon and its driver, rented for the occasion, await us downstairs. If I weren't ill, this trip would be a welcome distraction, but I'm worried about the danger we're running and—above all—about Mama, who seems increasingly feeble.

The driver warns my father one more time: "Remember, make sure you tell the checkpoint guards we're going to Jalalabad."

The road through the outlying district of Kabul is symbolic of the country's wartime history since the day I was born. It's strewn with the carcasses of Soviet tanks, and traces of the battles fought by the mujahideen when General Massoud's men took the city in 1992 are visible everywhere on the walls. Unexploded mines and rocket-propelled grenades are still buried in the rubble.

At the first checkpoint on the outskirts of the city, we must leave the car to show our papers and be frisked. The men are searched thoroughly in proper form: The guards attend to this themselves. For the women, the Taliban use little boys not much older than eight—these are the only males who may approach us. Since women may not work, there can be no policewomen.

The boy does not even speak to us; he simply gestures for us to lift up our *chadris*, runs his hand lightly over our long skirts, and quickly examines our faces to see that we have not broken the law against wearing makeup. That's it for us, as far as the search is concerned. The boy looks solemn, slightly disdainful, but he is probably very proud of his job in spite of his tender years. The weapon he wears slung over his shoulder is almost bigger than he is.

What kind of a man will he grow up to be?

Next comes the search of our baggage in the trunk.

My father points out his suitcase, which the guards open and carefully inspect.

"Where are you going?"

"To Jalalabad."

The fear of the travelers waiting here is oppressive, almost tangible. These Taliban are so unpredictable around women that anything can happen. In my mind I go over what I put in my suitcase: I took only black and dark clothes, nothing colorful. Mama and Soraya took the same precautions. In principle, women's baggage isn't searched, as the Taliban will not touch women's clothing.

In fact, my father has only to say, "This is my wife's suitcase, and these belong to my daughters," and the guard steps back.

There's a long line of cars behind and ahead of us; we must wait about twenty minutes before we can set out again. Bumps in the road are hurting my back, so Mama asks my father to tell the driver to slow down. The sun is climbing well up in the sky, and it's broiling hot. After two tiring hours on the road, we reach the town of Sarowbi, and go through a checkpoint exactly like the previous one. Then we drive off again along the same torturous road toward Jalalabad.

At the outskirts of the city, a third checkpoint. Each time, uneasiness makes us silently attentive to the guards' slightest gestures. They can bar our way or send us to prison without a word of explanation. If one of these men becomes angry at a single traveler for some infraction, everyone else will bear the consequences.

A bit farther on, we see a bus being searched. The Taliban make the women get out, then force the driver to turn the bus around.

The way the guards stare at my father and the suspicious looks they give the papers he shows them almost make me appreciate this *chadri*, even though the temperature in the sun is 104 degrees and I can hardly breathe.

Once we're past this checkpoint, we still need to tackle the mountain road that winds its way to Samarkhail, where a fourth checkpoint produces the same anxiety, the same fear of being arrested.

As we approach the pass at Turkham, on the border, we see little boys returning from Pakistan carrying cans of gas or oil or bags of sugar they will later resell. Men sitting on the ground offer afghanis to Pakistani travelers, and Pakistani rupees to Afghans.

It has taken us over seven hours to get this far, and Mama is utterly exhausted.

"They're going to close for the day, hurry," the driver warns us. "I'm not allowed to go any farther."

We must unload the suitcases, hail a boy with a handcart to transport them, and walk the rest of the way to the big, black, sinister metal gates that block the road ahead.

Papa and Soraya support Mama, helping her to walk. She advances slowly, too slowly, stopping at times to catch her breath. And we have no idea exactly when the guards close the border. Father must also keep an eye on the boy and his baggage cart, which is going too fast for us.

Ahead are the black gates, surrounded by concrete and barbed wire. It's impossible to cross the border any other way, except by climbing up a precipitous mountain path. In front of the gates, armed Taliban. On the other side, armed Pakistanis. Travelers go through in groups. We overhear people saying the gates will close between noon and one o'clock. We have a few minutes left, just enough time.

A *talib* rummages through our bags and examines my father's passport, the sole document attesting to the existence of his wife and daughters. It may be forbidden to leave the country, but the guard couldn't care less. Here, thousands of people cross over. What's important is that the travelers he's dealing with be a man and some properly silent and submissive women, their heads bowed beneath their *chadris*.

At that moment, a Pakistani policeman leaves his guard hut and prepares to close the border.

"Let us get through, my brother!" shouts a woman behind us. "Don't close the gates!"

The *talib* turns around, goes over to the Pakistani, and speaks to him so roughly that the man recoils without a word, and instead of going back inside his hut, he ducks behind it for fear the *talib* will shoot at him. Even he is afraid of them.

But he's not afraid of my father. As soon as we've crossed the border, he approaches him very self-importantly, with his weapon slung over his shoulder and a baton he holds out ostentatiously in front of him at arm's length like a barrier, grasping each end in a fist.

"Do you have a permit?"

My father hands him his passport. There is no permit required, and the Pakistani knows this. He doesn't want a document, he wants money.

"Where are you going?"

"To Peshawar. To seek medical attention for my wife and daughter."

My father resists, because he detests this business of giving money to an official who is not legally entitled to receive it. This territory really belongs to us, and the Pakistanis stole it. It's not their land, and they're so conscious of this that before they killed Najibullah, they tried to make him sign a document officially recognizing this illegal border. I know exactly what my father is thinking at this minute, in front of this Pakistani thief: "You're on my land, in *my* country, and you dare demand money from me, an Afghan! This is worse than a simple racket, this is an insult to Afghanistan!"

Everyone accepts the situation, the border is there, but that's exactly the point: Papa can't bear this acceptance and the fact that not one country in the world protested this theft. Finally, he pulls out a fifty-rupee bill. The guard shakes his head.

"That's not enough, it's fifty rupees each!"

Now my father is beside himself and raises his voice.

"What's that supposed to mean? What is it you want? Do you want me to create a disturbance here?"

The other man eventually gives in.

"Give me fifty," he says sourly. "All right. You can go."

Fifty Pakistani rupees, that's not a lot, about a dollar. But for my father it's a question of principle. In Kabul under the Taliban, the entire economy is based on cash, and Papa can obtain ready money only through his partner in Peshawar, to whom he loaned a modest sum for his business.

Papa is furious. After paying this blackmail, he mutters bitterly, "This is the *last* time I'm coming to Pakistan."

Now we must find a taxi to get to Peshawar. The driver we pick seems nice enough and immediately strikes up a conversation. In Kabul a taxi driver won't talk with his passengers; there's too much distrust everywhere.

"You're from Kabul?"

"Yes."

"I'm an Afghan, too. I've been living in Pakistan for eighteen years."

The car rolls along a free road, in a free world, and despite the heat, the mountainous terrain, and the sharp turns, the road is in much better shape than the one on the other side of the border. It's still dangerous, though; sometimes we catch a glimpse of a wrecked truck or bus at the bottom of a ravine.

But the slopes of the mountain are green, there are trees, and wildflowers bloom along the sides of the road. The driver stops for a moment by a cistern of clear water, which runs in sparkling channels down from the rocks above. There we can at last splash some cool water on our faces. I'm dying of suffocation, and so is Soraya. Our feet are swollen from the heat and from sitting so long. Lifting up my *chadri*, I sprinkle myself with this limpid water, which probably isn't safe to drink.

This short halt in the mountains is a real delight. I've had nothing to eat and very little to drink on our long trip. The water on my feverish cheeks is a gift from God, and to go about freely, without the Taliban, is a marvelous breath of oxygen. In spite of this feeling of freedom, though, our *chadris* will stay put until Peshawar, just to be safe.

"Me, I understand how you feel," says the driver, chatting with my father. "The situation in Afghanistan is a tragedy. The Taliban are bad people; they force too many things on you."

Papa asks him to drive slowly because of my mother,

who is ill, and we set out again. Soraya and I sit quietly, gazing at the countryside. The driver puts on some music, which wafts freely out the car's open windows, and at around two in the afternoon, we enter Peshawar through the neighborhood of Karkhana.

Before us stretch endless rows of shops several stories high, and the driver tells us about this immense bazaar stocked with all sorts of goods, products from around the entire world, a tribal zone without laws, taxes, or customs officials.

"Here you have the arms and drug merchants: All these stores sell nothing but that stuff. Farther on, at the checkpoint, you have your household items, cameras, televisions, radios, VCRs, air conditioners . . . whatever you want!"

Across the border, tribal networks import goods into Afghanistan without paying any customs duty, since we have none—or very little—in our country. The goods are then sent back into Pakistan, still without paying any taxes. Arms travel by the same route.

It's obvious that Pakistan is using our devastated country, ruined by years of civil war, as a convenient washing machine to "launder" merchandise. That's also why Pakistan speedily recognized the Taliban regime—many of whose fighters came from Pakistan, with the blessing of the United States.

We're done for if the resistance doesn't regain control

of the capital. Our country will be chewed up and swallowed down under cover of the perverse Sharia installed by the Taliban.

When we reach the home of Shakila's parents-in-law, my sister hugs us all, sobbing. She hasn't seen us for months and she has been worried sick about us. She was afraid she would have to join her husband in the United States without seeing us again first. In Peshawar, people know more or less what is going on in Kabul, but Shakila needs to hear what our daily life there is like.

"How can you bear to wear the *chadri*?"

"We don't go out."

"That's so hard for you, you're young. But what do you do at home?"

"I read; I try to go back to studying English with the books you sent me."

"Alone, or is Soraya helping you?"

"Alone, with the dictionary."

"You've gotten thin. And Mama as well—she's much too thin, and so weak."

Shakila asks about our uncles, aunts, and cousins as she sweeps us along to the bathrooms in the house. In *these* bathrooms (three of them!) the faucets produce running water, and we'll be able to take real showers, a luxury we no longer have in Kabul. Shakila and her sister-in-law bustle about, bringing us towels and soap.

Then Mama stretches out on a sofa, and Shakila gently massages her feet until she falls asleep, exhausted.

Shakila will soon be leaving for the United States. She's eager to be reunited with her husband, but doesn't know anything about the country. All she can tell us is that her husband has acquired a business in Virginia. To us, America is another world, and we're completely unfamiliar with its way of life, its people, the names of its cities. Shakila is heartsick at the thought of never seeing Afghanistan again, but she has confidence in her husband. She loves him.

Over in America, she will help out in her husband's store instead of being a journalist, but they will still observe our customs: She'll cover her head with a scarf to pray under a different sky, that's all.

Shakila tells me about my former classmates who now live in Peshawar. I think they're so lucky that they can go to the university here and continue their education.

We can't come live in Pakistan. Shakila will be leaving before long, and my father cannot possibly ask to stay with his oldest daughter's in-laws—he couldn't bear it.

The next day, at the hospital, I'm examined in one department, Mama in another. I have a chest X-ray.

"Why weren't you taken care of sooner?" the radiologist asks me.

I assume he knows that it's almost impossible for a

woman to receive medical care in Kabul. But he asks the questions anyway, as though it were our fault.

I'm hospitalized for a week. They tap my lungs, draining off two bottles of weird-looking fluid. I'm given B vitamins and some other medications I don't know the names of.

Papa visits me in the room I share with another patient and tells me about Mama.

"They've confirmed that she's severely diabetic," he says sadly. "To treat her depression, all the doctor could prescribe were some sedatives to relax her. He's keeping her two days, then I have to take her to a neurologist, because they don't have one here in the hospital."

So Mama leaves the hospital before I do, but her visit to the specialist is not reassuring. My father must try to explain to the doctor what she is unable to say for herself. He knows she will not speak of her inner suffering to anyone; she won't even talk to her own husband about it. And Papa doesn't dare go into detail about the series of nervous shocks she's had, either, because there are Pakistani guards on duty in front of the doctor's office, and an Afghan cannot feel free to speak under such conditions. There's always the risk of being overheard, and of getting into trouble with the regime.

Mama was happy before the Soviets came, enjoying both a flourishing career and a successful marriage. My parents' love for each other has never wavered, but they've had to weather so much misfortune and misery since the occupation. My oldest brother, Wahid, was denounced and imprisoned for three years. They had to hide their second son, Daoud, to save him from forcible conscription into the army. My mother lived through the horrors of the civil war every day, first as a nurse, then as a gynecologist. And now there is the suffering of all those women she has tried to help since the Taliban took over.

How can my father speak of what happened at Kabul University at the end of the fighting between the various factions of the mujahideen, a vicious struggle that lasted from 1993 to 1996?

I remember my mother's face perfectly as she listened to what Daoud had seen. I was twelve years old. It was so traumatizing that I have never been able to forget it.

At the time, Ahmed Shah Massoud had been battling Hekmatyar and his allies, who had closed the university and were using the buildings as a barracks. Hekmatyar lost, and when General Massoud's forces took control of that area, they appealed over the radio for the displaced students to come help clean up the premises so that they could be reopened. Daoud went to his university one morning along with many other students who had spontaneously responded to this appeal and were eager to resume their studies.

When he returned, Mama could tell immediately that

something was wrong: He was so pale and didn't want to talk. He shut himself up in his room without having any lunch.

Still in the kitchen, Mama called out, "Daoud, come eat!"

"No, I don't feel like it."

"What's the matter?"

Daoud wouldn't answer. We were worried, so I followed Mama into my brother's room. He was sitting on his bed, holding his head in his hands. Mama sat down next to him and waited until he could bring himself to speak.

"I saw something sickening, something really atrocious."

"What did you see?"

"There was a completely naked woman. . . . She was . . . nailed to a pair of swinging doors at the university, they'd sliced her in half . . . into two pieces. There was half of her body on each door . . . and the doors were opening and closing . . . It was terrifying."

Mama began to cry.

"They cut off people's hands and feet," continued Daoud. "There was bloody stuff lying all over the place. It was a massacre, Mama. I don't know how many they killed, but it was so awful. The radio just said that the students should help clean the university, straighten things up. But we couldn't clean it up, we couldn't. The security guards worked at it, but I don't want to go back there this afternoon, I just can't. They brought us over there so we could see what the other men did; they wanted us to know."

I went off to my room to cry by myself. Daoud never talked about this again, but I know Mama still thinks about it, I'm sure she does, and she has lots more nightmares in her head that I don't know about. Although she never mentions them, they're inside her, deeply buried.

Later, the newspapers reported that there had been a massacre at the university, but they didn't give any details.

The specialist advises my father to make certain that Mama takes her sedatives and her medication for the diabetes. He also wants him to make her walk for at least two hours a day.

After a week, I feel better. I can go out, and the doctor has advised me as well to walk for two hours a day, do exercises, and get as much fresh air as possible.

As my father told the doctor, "Aside from taking the pills, there's not much we can do back in Kabul."

In the evenings, at the home of Shakila's in-laws, we three sisters talk. It's a huge temptation to simply stay here, not to go back, to flee our country and that government that seems even more obscene from the outside.

But it's impossible. Shakila is leaving for the United States; she just spoke to her husband on the phone, and her papers are about to come through. Her in-laws can't keep us here. As for Soraya and me, it's unthinkable that our parents should go back to Afghanistan without us. Over there, we have a home, a reasonable rent that we can afford to pay. In Pakistan, we would be free, Mama would receive better care, I would attend the university, but as Shakila tells us, "Here, people don't really trust us. Even though all the businesses in Peshawar are run by Afghans—they build houses, they make the economy work—the Pakistanis still don't like us."

And it's true.

Meanwhile, I go out walking in the fresh air every other day. We've bought real shoes, black summer shoes to replace my sneakers, and fabrics to make some clothes, and Papa gave me a prayer scarf. Our family sits talking in the garden in the evening, enjoying the sunset. A real life.

At the end of a month, it's time to go home. Mama, Soraya, and I are desolate. I've seen my former classmates going to college, laughing and walking freely in the streets of Peshawar and Islamabad. Most of them have a brother, an uncle, some member of their immediate family living abroad who helps them financially, but that doesn't mean their life is luxurious. One girlfriend told me on the phone that there were seven of them in a single rented room in Islamabad. But she's lucky she can continue her studies—I hope she realizes this and works as hard as she did before. During our conversation, I had the feeling she wasn't as impatient to become a doctor as she once was; she seems more superficial now, less serious and socially concerned. Perhaps it's freedom that does that.

We make the trip home by bus, since Mama and I are doing better. The searches, the checkpoints, the Taliban with their evil looks, the usual humiliation. . . . I feel even more dispirited than I did before we left Kabul.

Mama refuses to take the medications for her diabetes. My father and Soraya think up all kinds of tricks to get her to swallow the medicine. She prefers tranquilizers and sleeping pills. We watch over her as if she were a child. My mother, once so strong and active, has turned her back on reality. She erases it in a deeper and deeper sleep. The four of us are at our wit's end. Her depression is spreading to the rest of us.

And we're even more aghast when Daoud tells us that instead of the soccer he so loved, there's a new sport in the stadium in Kabul. Now the Taliban use the place as a public execution ground: They hang their prisoners from the goalposts, cut off the hands of thieves, put a bullet in the back of the heads of women accused of adultery. A monstrous spectacle, periodically interrupted for obligatory prayers. They force people to watch by beating them with whips.

I can't take it. I don't want to hear any more about the horrors in our city.

I won't leave the apartment again. I'll just look out the kitchen window, and sleep as much as I can, like Mama, to forget what Kabul has become: a nightmare in broad daylight.

FOUR

Massacres and Miracles

It's 8:30 P.M.: time for the BBC. Papa turns on the big radio, setting the volume very low, and we gather around the way we always do, sitting as close as possible to the speaker. One day, our next-door neighbor told Soraya that he had heard our radio.

"You've got it on too loud, and they say that the Taliban . . ."

Soraya interrupted him quickly, prudently pretending to apologize for any inconvenience we had caused.

"My sister and I were listening to music—we're sorry if it was too loud!"

The neighbor never mentioned it again, but to be on the safe side, we're even more careful now. We practically hug the speaker, listening to the bulletin.

"Mazar-i-Sharif, an important city in northern Afghanistan, has for more than a year been the site of terrific fighting between the Taliban and the mujahideen of the Northern Alliance. The Taliban's efforts to take the city, where they have suffered heavy losses since their entry into Kabul, have so far been in vain, but if they can win Mazar-i-Sharif, then the last of the resistance strongholds in the north will have fallen."

So the BBC confirms what's being whispered around Kabul, rumors that we can never wholly believe. Even when a reporter manages to interview someone from one side or the other, it's hard to get a clear idea of the situation. Whatever claims the Taliban regime makes are immediately denied by the leaders of the resistance. Sometimes the broadcast is inaudible. In the morning, for example, between 5:30 and 7:30, when Iranian radio is on the air, the sound is completely garbled. In Kabul they say that the Taliban jam the program on purpose, because it covers the mujahideen's advances. Of course, anyone in Kabul caught listening to the broadcast risks spending three months in prison.

The news has been demoralizing lately. In February 1998, an earthquake struck the north of the country, in the area of Taloqan, with tremors felt as far away as Tajikistan, and it was the BBC that gave us the toll: four thousand dead.

But it's Radio Sharia that brings us news of the Taliban's supreme justice: Two criminals have had their throats cut in the Kabul sports stadium by the father of their victims, before a large crowd estimated by the Taliban at 35,000 people. Fortunately they don't use television to bring us this entertainment in the comfort of our own homes. On such occasions I don't mind not having TV anymore.

My mother is particularly worried about the news that the Taliban have expelled from Kabul a humanitarian organization that was essentially managed by women. It represented the last opportunity for Afghan women to have access to medical services. The women who ran it were accused of not obeying the Islamic prohibition against work, education, and even health care for women. Mama is devastated.

"It's all over for women. Finished. There's nothing left. It's genocide. And the United Nations goes along with the fraud perpetrated by those men!"

Soraya is sad, and doesn't say much anymore. She tries to keep busy around the apartment. Papa tells her over and over that she won't lose her job skills, that she'll be able to go back to work one day, but she doesn't believe it anymore. No one cares about us; journalists have become so rare you'd think the whole world had forgotten us and that other countries approved of the Taliban.

In August 1998, Radio Sharia, to which we can listen in the morning without worrying about the neighbors, announces triumphantly the capture of Mazar-i-Sharif, not far from the borders of Tajikistan and Uzbekistan. The Taliban have invaded the holy city, whose blue mosque shelters the tomb of Ali,* the Prophet's son-in-law.

"Thanks to God who is great, we are unifying the country! All the cities in the north have rejoined the government!"

Radio Iran then attacks the United States, accusing it of supporting the Taliban in an effort to soil the image of Islam. The Taliban have massacred hundreds of civilians in the holy city and kidnapped Iranian diplomats in the name of a religion that would never condone such barbarism.

"They preach jihad," observes my father, "but a Muslim does not kill another Muslim. Nowhere does it say in the Koran that one should take another life. This is the proof that they make up their own *Sharia,* trying to persuade us that everything they decide is written in the Koran. Their laws aren't written, they're concocted by a few mullahs who ought to keep them to themselves."

I go lie down next to Soraya, who is sleeping with her pretty face shrouded in the sheet, in spite of the heat. And I think about Mazar-i-Sharif, about the wonderful trip Wahid organized when I was around twelve years old: the first trip I'd ever taken in Afghanistan—and so far, the last, too. I was thrilled to go off with Mama, Shak-

*The Prophet's son-in-law is the greatest saint of the Shiite sect of Islam, and this shrine gives its name to Mazar-i-Sharif, which means "noble tomb." [translator's note]

ila, and my big brother, whom I so admired! Papa stayed home with Soraya, because they both had to work. We were going to be celebrating Nowroz, the Afghan New Year, which begins on the first day of spring, in the city of the tomb of Ali, and we planned to stay there for a month.

I remember a place along the road where uniformed men were looking through the baggage of all travelers. One of these men asked our driver where we were going.

"To Mazar-i-Sharif, to the great mosque."

The man held out a cash box. "Contribute!"

The driver put a few bills into the box without a word, and we drove on.

Wahid had hired the driver and his car for the entire trip. The man was quite nice and told us that he'd be glad to stop if we wanted to look at anything or go to the bathroom.

At the beginning of our trip, there wasn't anything to see except the desert on either side. While I was looking out the window, I noticed two young men a little taller than I was, probably about fourteen years old, with Kalashnikovs. When our driver did not slow down, one of the boys threw himself in front of the car, waving us to a halt.

"Why didn't you stop?"

"I didn't know you wanted me to!"

"Pull over to the side of the road and give us some money!"

So the driver shelled out a little more money to these boys.

"If you're thirsty," he told us later, "I'll stop after the pass at Salang and the tunnel. I advise you to drink the water there; it comes from the mountain."

The water was marvelous, cool and clear, and the landscape was magnificent. There were houses clinging to the mountainside, and people going up and down on a narrow path that wound through the trees all the way to the top of the peak. We ate delicious mutton kebabs; the driver claimed that the north offered the best food in all Afghanistan.

After lunch, we drove on, and just before we reached Pol-i-Khomri, I saw the house of my dreams, the one I used to draw when I was little: a gray stone house in a lovely natural setting, surrounded by greenery, with a sheepfold, a well, and curls of smoke coming from the chimney. I would have liked to live there in the valley, amid the trees, in the peace and quiet. It was so beautiful. Wahid told me that the next village we would be driving through was Dasht-i-Kilaguyi, which means *banana*.

"You often talk to us about Dasht-i-Kilaguyi."

"So there are lots of bananas there?"

"Well, no, actually, but there *are* lots of watermelons!"

The driver joined the conversation, asking Wahid to

give him his watch, and Mama's too. "If anybody's got a watch, better let me have it."

When Mama asked him why, he replied, "Madam, if you have any jewelry, you must give it to me, because we'll soon be in a place where thieves can stop the car and strip us of everything."

After hiding the watches and jewelry in the trunk, he drove quickly on, warning us, "If someone throws a stone, don't worry, I won't stop."

I did see some robbers along the way, but they were already busy with another car.

Outside the city, there was a huge banner: "Welcome to Mazar-i-Sharif."

The people were all Uzbeks in traditional clothing, thick brown shirts called *gopitchas* and round turbans wound from very long cloths. I'd already seen a few Uzbeks in Kabul, but that day everyone I saw seemed to have the same slightly Mongol features. The women weren't all wearing the *chadri;* some wore scarves, others no head covering at all.

We went to a hotel to rest from our trip. So many people were in town that almost everything was taken, but after arguing with the proprietor, Wahid managed to get us a room big enough for four people.

Wahid could be somewhat overbearing. Sometimes he quarreled with Shakila, and they wouldn't speak to each other for two or three days. My parents wouldn't know anything about it—my sister didn't want to bother

Mama with such things, which were just between her and Wahid. With me, Wahid was different. He would take me to the amusement park, to the dodgem cars, and he was always teasing me and my girl cousins. He would show us postcards of glamorous Indian movie stars lit up with a flashlight and make us pay five afghanis each, as though we were at the movies. Or else he would invent bank accounts for himself and ask us to entrust our money to him in return for a fake checkbook. Daoud laughed and called him a thief, because we all knew he was trying to hustle up some pocket money to go to the movies after school. He was twenty-five when we went to Mazar-i-Sharif. He's changed since then. His face is always sad and serious, and Mama says he has simply suffered too much.

I feel as though my brother sums up the history of the war in Afghanistan, since he's the soldier in the family.

He studied at Ansari High School, then at the military academy. He was the best officer cadet in his class, and was assigned to the presidential guard regiment. To complete his training, the Soviets sent him to the front for the first time, with a unit operating at Maidan Shahr. He was there for about three weeks. At that time, the most active fronts were those at Kandahar, Maidan Shahr, and Wardak. When he returned, he told us that Soviet soldiers massacred civilians openly in front of Afghan troops, that they shot children and old people for no reason. In some villages, when women threw pebbles at them, they shot back with their Kalashnikovs. Wahid was deeply shaken by this experience, and Mama told me she had wept more than once, listening to his stories. Each time he returned to the front, she would say sadly, "He goes off as if he were committing suicide."

In two years, he took part in more than 104 operational missions—and was also confined to barracks several times for insubordination. His punishment would be to spend a few days in a campaign tent, which is very small and low and is pitched over the damp, bare ground. You had to either huddle down or stretch out flat inside. Wahid's commanding officer at the time was Colonel Hazrat, his instructor, who constantly extolled the merits of Soviet aid in Afghanistan and demanded that his men blindly obey Soviet orders. But Wahid rebelled against the Russians' orders, often challenging his instructors. He used to tell us, "Afghanistan has enough men and officers—we don't need the Soviets!" Once, when we hadn't heard from him for weeks, Mama sent Daoud to the barracks, where he learned that our older brother had been sentenced to five months' confinement for throwing a teapot at his colonel's head. After that, he was transferred to another unit, at Paghman, at the edge of the buffer zone west of Kabul.

One day an old man, a mullah from the elders' council out there, came to see our father at home: "I've come to thank you for the valuable services your son is performing for us."

When he saw Wahid come home on leave, put on traditional clothing, and wear the Afghan *pakol* in the apartment, Papa certainly realized what was going on, but he questioned Wahid anyway.

"Why did the mullah of Paghman come to thank me?"

Why indeed . . . Wahid was in charge of security for that part of the buffer zone around Kabul. After the victory against the Soviets, the Afghan resistance controlled almost all the countryside, and the Communist government in Kabul tried principally to defend the large cities, the main roads, and the airports. Hundreds of soldiers held positions in the hills surrounding the capital. Normally, the army did not allow villagers to cross this buffer zone to purchase provisions in Kabul, but Wahid would let them through. Unfortunately, the government secret police, the Khad, got wind of this. Wahid was called before General Farouq Yaqubi, second-in-command in the Khad. And my brother proudly explained his actions to him.

"The army taught me to serve the people. I allow the representatives of the people to go through. If you object, then replace me with whoever informed on me!"

He wasn't punished that day. I suppose his answer was rather embarrassing to a Soviet, in theory a defender of the people. But Wahid knew that he was now under surveillance by the redoubtable Khad, that copy of the Soviet KGB.

In reality, he had been approached by the resistance, because his responsibility for the Paghman sector of the buffer zone around Kabul made him a valuable contact.

After two years of active service on the front, he was transferred for two months to a military base at Fronze, in Kirghizstan. Each weekend, my brother would come home, take off his uniform, slip into traditional native costume, put on his *pakol,* and go off to the mosque to pray.

One day, a man named Sangar, who lived in the building next door in Mikrorayan and was the brother-in-law of President Najibullah, stopped Wahid in the street. Nine years old at the time, I was with my parents out on our balcony, and from our perch we watched them talk for almost two hours.

My father was worried, because Sangar was not only close to President Najibullah, he was also in charge of one branch of the Khad. As soon as Wahid came home, we bombarded him with questions.

"Well, what did he tell you?"

"What did he want?"

"Nothing! It was nothing much, just small talk. Don't worry. . . ."

He was evasive, trying to reassure us, but shortly afterward he disappeared, and we had no news of him for more than three weeks. We figured he'd been sent somewhere without having had the time to let us know, but one summer evening a soldier from his unit came discreetly to see us. He spoke to Shakila and left, and when I pleaded with her to tell me what they'd talked about, all she would say was, "We have to wait for Papa."

Finally, at dinner, Shakila gave us the news: "Wahid is in prison."

Papa was furious that the army had not told us anything. He telephoned Hashim, a family friend, who worked in the personnel department of the Khad, and they made an appointment to go looking together for Wahid the next morning.

General Issa Khan, commandant of the garrison of Paghman and the head of Wahid's unit, told them that he was being held in cell block 2 of Pol-i-Sharkhi, which was reserved for political prisoners. We were in despair. It was the worst thing that had ever happened to our family. Wahid, a political prisoner of the Russians . . .

The first time my father went to the prison he was not allowed to see his son. The guard on duty was only able to accept some clean clothes for my brother, and he agreed to hand over Wahid's dirty laundry to my father.

In the lining of the trousers, Wahid had hidden a scrap of paper on which he had written: "Father, I am alive. You must obtain a letter of authorization from the Minister of Security to see me. Wahid."

It took Hashim almost a month to get a signed letter

from the minister granting the entire family the right to visit Wahid. We heard horrendous rumors about Pol-i-Sharkhi Prison. One of my maternal uncles, Mir Akbar, had been incarcerated there during the 1970s and had told us how he'd been tortured, how his nails had been torn off and his back cut to ribbons. Pol-i-Sharkhi was quite different from the old prison in Kabul, built of bricks and earth; this one was a real Soviet fortress, constructed when the Communists took over.

When we came out onto that plain lying about nine miles from Kabul, I could see in the distance a massive citadel with walls so wide that a car could have driven around on top of them. Hundreds of visitors were lined up to see a family member inside. I was dumbfounded, wondering why there were so many people in prison.

Two hundred yards from the entrance, two huts sheltered the police officers assigned to supervise the visitors: one was reserved for women, the other for men. After waiting for an hour, we heard our name. My mother, sisters, and I entered the women's hut, where a woman marked our arms with a rubber stamp. Papa received the same stamp in the men's hut.

The woman searched us, then allowed us to proceed to the immense metal door, so tall that I had to lean back to read the two inscriptions above it: "State Prison of the Democratic Republic of Afghanistan" and "Prison is the second school of life."

What did they mean by that? I didn't understand what one might learn in prison.

Every time we went to see Wahid, not only did we have to line up to be stamped before we could be searched, but the same procedure was repeated inside the prison, where we went through six metal doors like that. At each one, the guards checked the marks on the men's arms and signed right on their skin in confirmation. When he reached the end of the corridor, my father had two stamps and six signatures on his arm.

Next we were led into a courtyard open to the sky in the center of the building. The ground was sprinkled with water to keep the dust down. They loudly called my brother's name, and at last he appeared. He stretched a shawl out over the ground for us to sit on. I couldn't take my eyes off him. He wore a beard and was dressed in black. We were all in tears while Wahid kissed our parents' hands and begged us not to cry. We had only a half hour together, and he had much to tell us, but we were watched by an armed soldier who listened to the conversation, so Wahid could only explain the most important things.

He had already been interrogated. He needed a lawyer for his trial, and he wanted our uncle, Mir Akbar, to defend him. He urged my sisters always to wear the chador, as well as long traditional dresses like the ones we were wearing that day. As usual, he was very emphatic about that, but this time Shakila didn't argue with him over it. Finally, before he left us, Wahid hugged his sisters and whispered to us, "Some men will be guarding the house. Don't be afraid. There are three of them, and they are there to protect you."

He gave us his dirty laundry, and we left without having discovered what the specific charges against him were and why men would be watching closely over us.

My uncle was a prosecutor in a military court, so he was perfectly familiar with army regulations. And because he had been incarcerated there, he knew the rules of prison life. When he came to our home, the first thing he asked was if we had picked up Wahid's dirty laundry. He immediately rummaged through the bundle and found pieces of paper in the creases of the trousers. Wahid had written personally to ask our uncle to come see him in prison as soon as possible, insisting that he wanted no other lawyer but him. I found this system of communication astounding.

From then on, every Wednesday for three months, we went to see my brother in prison in that courtyard of damp and greasy beaten earth. Wahid said that the guards threw water on it to wash away traces of blood. There were some stains on the walls as well. Much later, after Massoud's mujahideen arrived in Kabul, they showed us a terrifying report on television. When they dug up this greasy dirt, they uncovered the corpses of prisoners who had been summarily executed. So we had actually been walking, without realizing it, on a mass grave.

Each time we visited him, Wahid told us stories about the prison. There was a head guard, ready to offer special privileges in exchange for money: Commandant Khiali Gul. And in fact, this man came to see my father in his store, pocketed some money, and that very night, Wahid telephoned us at home. He was able to speak with us for a long time, from the commandant's own room. He asked for a small TV set—which amazed us because we thought such things weren't allowed—and an antenna with an extension cord thirty yards long to run from his cell to the prison roof! And he was able to install this TV without any trouble.

Once, in the courtyard, he pointed out a prisoner to us.

"His name is Ghazi, he's the prison killer. For five thousand afghanis, he agrees to shoot the condemned prisoners. I was told that General Abdul Wahid, one of the top commanders of the resistance, was captured during an offensive in the Panshir Valley and executed by Ghazi."

One fall day, when rain was coming down in torrents, a squad of armed soldiers suddenly invaded the prison. A detainee had managed to escape disguised as a woman beneath a long *chadri.*

At the exit, the guards peered at all the women before letting them through, and armored vehicles were parked in front of the gates. At our next visit, we women were treated to two stamps on the arm instead of one, and Wahid told us that the escaped prisoner had made fake stamps with potatoes and a felt-tip pen his wife had brought him. On the outside, he had specialized in forging documents.

During a riot among political prisoners in rival resistance factions who were housed on the same floor, a new arrival was murdered, stabbed with blades crafted from sharpened slivers of bone. Prisoners used to pick over the kitchen garbage dumped in a corner of the courtyard, looking for something to turn into a weapon.

An inmate was scalded to death when another prisoner threw boiling water in his face. Another man, in cell block 4, the one that housed the toughest criminals, had the bright idea of setting his clothes on fire with gasoline and dashing into the prison courtyard in hopes that his action would win him the sympathetic attention of the International Red Crescent. He planned to jump into a tub of water he knew was kept behind a door, but the door was locked that day, and the other prisoners watched through the bars as he burned alive. And then there was that young detainee, eighteen years old, arrested for theft, whom one of the men in block 4 served up to his pals for a gang rape. The older man worked in the kitchen. His victim took revenge by cutting his throat with a cleaver.

Shakila listened to my brother's stories with the curiosity of a journalist; Soraya often wept, while I wondered in what godforsaken world these men all lived.

One day Shakila invited a clairvoyant, the mother of a friend of hers, to come to our apartment. After handling my brother's clothing and making complicated calculations based on his date of birth, she announced: "Wahid is a wise and pious man, a good Muslim who says his prayers. In four months, he will be set free!"

She seemed so convinced of this that Mama was impressed and wanted to pay the woman, but our guest refused.

"Until my prediction has come true, I ask for nothing."

I didn't believe one bit of it. And Papa simply said that it was good for Mama's morale.

It was January 1992. Wahid had been condemned to twenty years in prison, a sentence my uncle had managed to have reduced to eighteen years. Wahid had been in Pol-i-Sharkhi for almost three years, and I tried to imagine what could ever get him out of there, aside from God's own mercy.

My sisters and I prayed fervently for his freedom.

On April 18, 1992, the head of the Khad, General Baqi, and his deputy director, General Yaqoubi, both close associates of Najibullah, were assassinated.

I was in school when Shakila came to ask permission to take me home. She knew that something was going on and that it was safer to be back at the apartment. News traveled fast in Mikrorayan, where many members of the Afghan Communist Party lived. Besides, the neighborhood is both close to the presidential palace and situated between the radio station and the international airport. And Shakila was a reporter, after all.

That evening, when we turned on the television, all we found were patriotic songs. At around 7:30, an anchorman came on and read a communiqué.

"My fellow countrymen, Dr. Najibullah, the former president who attempted to leave Afghanistan illegally," and so on and so forth. "In order to avoid a power vacuum and to keep the fate of our country out of the hands of the Pakistanis, we are in constant contact with the mujahideen. . . ."

At the time, we weren't sure exactly whom the government had contacted to fill the power vacuum. And then one morning, while Shakila and I were shopping, the vegetable merchant said, "General Massoud will enter Kabul. The whole city is talking about it!"

What everyone dreaded was the arrival in Kabul of

forces loyal to Massoud's rival, Hekmatyar, because they were the ones shooting rockets at us.

The Minister of Foreign Affairs appeared on the television news program the following evening.

"I flew by helicopter to the Panshir Valley to negotiate the transfer of power. Gulbuddin Hekmatyar and Ahmed Shah Massoud have agreed to enter Kabul without any hostilities."

At school the next day, I noticed quite a few changes. Our teachers were wearing big chadors or long coats and pants instead of skirts and pantyhose. The girls were all talking about the previous evening's newscast.

"If Hekmatyar's extremists take power, the war will keep going."

"Things will change for women, they won't be able to work anymore."

"Girls' schools will be closed down."

I didn't dare say much because my brother was in prison and I didn't want anything I said to cause trouble for him, but I was afraid that Wahid shared the views of the extremists.

Two days later, we noticed uniformed men in our neighborhood. Some of them had even stationed themselves in a corner of our school. Since they were in army uniforms, my classmates didn't think they could be mujahideen.

That same day, some of our neighbors, especially

those who worked in the Ministry of the Interior, began bringing various things home with them: TV sets, weapons, VCRs, cassettes. The looting seemed to have begun. Men started letting their beards grow.

Television broadcasts continued much as before, with male or female announcers. There was still music. But on the evening of April 28, the anchorwoman, although she was still wearing makeup, had already put on a headscarf. That was something new to us. A few days later, Sibghatullah Modjaddedi was declared the President of the Islamic State of Afghanistan.*

On May 5, the prison gates swung open: Political prisoners and criminals were all set free at the same time.

That evening, Wahid came home. Bearded, wearing traditional clothing, he knew more about what was happening than we did, even though he had only just gotten out of prison. We were all overjoyed to be together again, but the next morning he went to the market to buy us three huge chadors that were nothing like the scarves we were used to wearing.

*After they captured Kabul in April 1992 and proclaimed Afghanistan an Islamic state, the mujahideen ruled the nation through several councils, including the Resolution and Settlement Council. Modjaddedi was the first man to occupy the revolving presidency; when his brief term was up, Burhanuddin Rabbani succeeded him at the end of 1992 but later refused to relinquish office in his turn. A peace accord between Rabbani and Hekmatyar collapsed, fighting between rival mujahideen forces escalated, and the Taliban began their rise to power. [translator's note]

That was when Shakila told him bitterly, "Of course we'll wear your chadors—they're the *latest* fashion!"

It was the following year that we left on our pilgrimage to Mazar-i-Sharif to celebrate the Afghan New Year, which coincides there with Gul-e-sorkh, the festival of red tulips.

When we reached Mazar-i-Sharif, we saw a fantastic sight, whole fields of long-stemmed red tulips, a truly delightful living collection for Soraya. I'd never seen such a thing: a bloodred ocean gleaming in the sunshine all around the city.

We visited the great mosque with its blue dome, saw the ancient ornamental basin with stones engraved with verses from the Koran. The marble pavement of the courtyard was sky blue flecked with dark red, as smooth as a magic mirror, with white doves all around the edges. On New Year's Day, it was decorated with pots of red tulips. It was really superb.

Some blind or crippled pilgrims had been praying there for a year, waiting to attend this New Year's festival and ask for a miracle that day.

Inside the mosque there was a large Koran, lying open on a lectern, for the faithful to leaf through in search of verses to recite, but I saw people who recited from memory, without consulting the holy book. We made a donation to the mosque and went to pray at the shrine of Ali. Shakila asked a woman what we should do next and was told: "This is the temple of Ali. You may pray and ask God for something. Your wish will come true—he works miracles."

I prayed for Mama to be healthy, and for God to protect my whole family. Then we noticed something strange: hundreds of padlocks hanging from a metal bar, all of them locked. I couldn't figure out what they could possibly be for. When we asked another woman, she told us, "You must choose a padlock at random and pull on it: If it opens, your wish will be granted. My sister-in-law did that a few days ago; she asked for her husband to return to Mazar-i-Sharif, because she was worried about him. He came home that very evening!"

Shakila refused to pull on a padlock. I would have been glad to do it; I even reached out to touch one, but my sister stopped me.

"I don't know what this is all about, Latifa! I've never seen this before, and to avoid making a mistake and breaking some rule, we'd better not touch them."

Wahid had prayed in the part of the mosque reserved for men and was waiting for us outside.

We bought birdseed to feed the doves of the blue mosque. I noticed that there were many foreigners, even some Westerners amazed by the splendor of this mosque. There are mosques in Kabul that are just as big and just as beautiful, but this one is unique, and particularly venerated because it contains the tomb of Ali, who can work miracles.

And by some strange chance, Shakila and I witnessed a miracle.

Some men had raised a flag over the enormous crowd. The sick and handicapped were praying directly in front of us. Suddenly, a man lifted his arms to the sky, rubbing his eyes and shouting like a madman that he'd just recovered his sight. People around him immediately began tearing off shreds of his clothing, which had become holy, while the man kept thanking God, rubbing at his face, and staring at the heavens in ecstasy, letting the faithful press in closer and closer around him. I could see hands stretched out to him, begging respectfully, yet insistently; I was actually afraid that he would wind up with no more cloth to give them. But he didn't even notice the seething excitement surrounding him, and dazzled by the light, he kept placing his hands over his eyes, then removing them, weeping and calling out, "Thank you, God!" His family protected him as best they could.

I was stunned. Pulling Shakila's sleeve, I kept saying: "Look! Look! It's a miracle!"

"I *am* looking—let go, you're hurting me."

Mama was too far from us at that moment to share our astonishment, but she saw what happened, and she also believed it was a miracle. Later, a man who worked at the mosque told us that this pilgrim had been waiting in front of the mosque for a year, praying every day.

Wahid was impressed as well, but much calmer than we were. "God is truly great," he said solemnly.

I told this marvelous story to my father as soon as we returned home to Kabul.

"I've seen a miracle, too," he said. "A man with a paralyzed leg began to walk right before my eyes. Miracles often happen in Mazar-i-Sharif."

Tonight, on August 12, 1998, I cannot fall asleep. They're already talking about massacres in the holy city. There will be hundreds of dead.

The tulips have faded since the spring; the Taliban will not have seen the flowers opening their bloodred petals to the sun. The Taliban themselves have shed the blood of the men and women of Mazar-i-Sharif. "God is truly great," Wahid had said, "and thanks to the intercession of Ali, the blind can see again."

If I could make one prayer to Ali before his marble tomb in the blue mosque, I would implore him to work one more miracle for the Afghan people, abandoned by everyone.

I would pray that these Taliban—who in their ignorance of the Koran dare invent laws that are inhuman and contrary to sacred scripture—learn to respect the holy book, humbly, as we Afghans do, and have always done.

FIVE

Three Little Girls from Taimani

This morning I'm preparing tea in the kitchen for my friend Farida, who has come down from the sixth floor to talk to me. She thinks that I'm too passive, that I'm not taking care of myself. My fever is gone, my lungs are better, and for some time now Farida has been nagging me to snap out of my depression and apathy. She always has some good excuse to come give me a pep talk and cheer me up. She goes outside occasionally, whereas I'm still dragging myself aimlessly around the apartment, dejected over Mama's illness and Soraya's sadness. We open the kitchen window to let in a little air, and through the grating, I look out at the mosque, as I often do. They've finished their construction work there, perhaps with funds from that Osama bin Laden I wrote about for my exam.

The mosques have become the domain of the Taliban, where they teach their version of the Koran. I can see the mullah in the center of the courtyard, surrounded by little boys endlessly reciting under his supervision. He's holding a stick, this mullah, probably to strike any child who hesitates or makes a mistake.

Farida watches him too.

"Maybe he's making them recite dreadful things! Look at that poor boy, he's smacking his hands."

It's at this precise moment, watching them out the window, that something clicks in my brain. First of all, of course, there are no girls, only boys, in that Koranic school. And these children can learn only one thing from a mullah: the texts of the Koran. Religious education is important; it has always been one of my courses, but I've been taught a wealth of other things as well: history, geography, Persian literature, mathematics, science. Who is going to teach the children all that now? There are still schools for boys; they aren't compulsory, although some parents must think that a minimum of education is better than nothing. But what kind of education is this? Taliban propaganda sneaks in there so quickly! During their first three years of school, boys have to wear little hats and what looks like pajamas. When they're eight or nine years old, they must begin wearing the white turban, which is way too big for them.

Lots of boys in the neighborhood don't go to school anymore because their parents don't want them indoctrinated by the Taliban. Other children, whose mothers are widows, get absolutely no education because they're out in the street begging or selling anything at all to help their mothers. For these women outside the system, their sons are their only means of survival.

Compared to all these children, I've been very lucky, after all. My own education wasn't interrupted until the Taliban arrived. I attended primary school when I was five, during the Soviet occupation; I was nine when the civil war between the mujahideen and the Communist regime began, and twelve when it ended, but it did not seriously disrupt my studies; and under the Islamic state government established by the resistance, I finished high school and began taking the entrance exams for the journalism department at the university.

Now I'm eighteen, and for two years I've been living shut up within these walls doing nothing, when I could perhaps make myself useful by joining those who are passing on their knowledge, even though I consider my learning somewhat skimpy.

This morning, Farida agrees with me; maybe she's been thinking the same thing for a while now.

"Listen, Latifa: It's over for you and me, at this point. We'll never go any further with our education, but we could do something for those children. They should at least have some idea how to evaluate what that mullah is telling them."

"An underground school? Like Mrs. Fawzia had?"

One of our former teachers was recently caught by the Taliban right in the middle of a class. First they beat the children, then they attacked her, throwing her so violently down the stairs of her building that they broke one of her legs. Then they dragged her off by the hair, threw her in prison, and forced her to sign a statement saying that she would never disobey Taliban law again. They threatened to stone her entire family in public if she didn't confess her "error."

I admire that woman immensely. She taught us so much when I was a student! When she created her secret school, Mrs. Fawzia knew what she was doing and the risk she was taking. The children never arrived at the same hour to take her classes and never left all at the same time. They kept their books at her home, so that nothing illegal—according to the decrees of the Taliban—would be seen outside. She must have been denounced and exposed by a neighbor or a street beggar. These last are always sniffing around for something with which they hope to curry favor with the authorities in Kabul. It is such a shame, because Mrs. Fawzia was so careful. At the beginning of every class, she would tell the children, "Keep a copy of a sura from the Koran next to you on the table. If anyone enters the room, you must say that we're busy studying it, and that it's the only thing we're working on!"

The mosque and those little boys reciting as they rock back and forth, hypnotized or terrorized by the mullah—that's the jolt I needed this morning to spring into action. Sometimes things happen like that—it's just fate.

Farida suggests that I replace Mrs. Fawzia and continue her work. Our former teacher would thus have her little revenge, knowing that someone was picking up where she was forced to leave off. So Farida and I talk seriously about setting up our school according to the principles of our predecessor.

"She needs to give us a course program, and tell us what she has already covered."

"We should take students only from our sector of apartment buildings, from families we know well, whom we can trust."

"We'll have to ask our girlfriends to help us. Maryam, for example—I'm sure she'd jump at the chance."

"Each of us will hold classes in her own apartment. Spreading things out will help keep what we're doing secret."

Finally, I have work to do! We write a short note to Mrs. Fawzia that we send to her through discreet channels, because it's safer not to go see her at home or to ask her to come here. In any case, the unfortunate woman has not recovered from her injuries and has trouble getting around.

She quickly sends word to us that she accepts our

offer with joy, adding that not only will she give us her lesson programs, she will also come help us out from time to time. Considering what she has already suffered, we think she's extraordinarily courageous.

Feeling confident, I tell my father and Daoud about our plan. Farida does the same with her father and Saber. We cannot succeed without the approval of our families, who must agree to receive these pupils illegally in their homes.

Everyone supports us, but Daoud has a word of warning.

"It's great that Mrs. Fawzia is giving you her lesson plans, but if she risks arousing suspicion by coming here, then you're taking a grave responsibility for her life. If the Taliban catch her a second time, she's done for. Finished! You haven't the right to do that to her."

Our two families then agree that Mrs. Fawzia should not come here to help out. As soon as she can send us her lesson plans, however, we'll get our organization up and running.

I take eight children, and Farida does the same. Maryam will have five, on average, depending on what day it is. Our pupils will be between five and fourteen years old, both girls and boys. We're taking risks as well, of course, but we're careful to limit them: The children won't have far to walk to get here, since they will simply be coming from inside the same building, which has thirty-six apartments, or from the immediate neighborhood. This proximity is vital for their safety. One of my girl cousins, who lives in Taimani, a neighborhood in Kabul, told my father a story that affected us terribly and underscored the need for such precautions. In Taimani there was a clandestine school for little girls, but they had to walk half an hour to get there, which was tremendously dangerous for them. One day, the bodies of several of the girls, seven or eight years old, were discovered in a garbage dump. They had been kidnapped, raped, and strangled with their own clothing. I often think of the little girls of Taimani while we set up our own school, and in their memory, I'm determined to do my best to help our neighborhood children.

In spite of her weakness, Mama feels energized and helps us out as well. I try to protect her as much as possible from the noise, because the children come and go at different times, and the disturbance is tiring for her. But I think she appreciates our effort even more since she herself can't practice her own profession.

Soraya has promised to correct the children's written work in the evening. Daoud takes care of obtaining basic materials such as pencils and notebooks, and each family gives us money to pay for these supplies. The only real problem is books. We can find them, but they're so expensive: 12,000 afghanis for a simple textbook, an enormous sum, given the inflation rampant in our country. So the pupils' parents buy one manual for each child, according to their means.

Maryam teaches mathematics. Farida and I handle reading, history, and composition. Another girlfriend specializes in English for the older students.

After our morning classes, I study the street out the window. If I see anyone I don't recognize or who seems suspicious, the children wait before leaving. Often, they even have lunch here. Then I let the biggest boys go first. After another check of the street, the girls go off together, along with one girl's young brother. Oddly enough, I'm not frightened. I do my work calmly, and so do my friends. Our network is airtight, we know all the parents personally, and the children are motivated and perfectly aware of the secret they must keep, the purpose of our improvised school, and its importance to them in the intellectual desert of the Taliban regime. They don't carry anything on them when they leave the apartment—no books at all, not the smallest notebook, not even a pencil. I keep everything in my room. And they come to class empty-handed as well, as if they were simply walking from one building to another, all at different times.

I begin working between nine and ten in the morning, depending on who has arrived, and classes stop at noon. I teach in my room: religious studies, history and geography, Persian literature, and twice a week, writing and dictation.

I have five girls: Ramika is fourteen; she's the only one who wears the *chadri*. Kerechma and Tabasom are two seven-year-old twins; Malika is six; and Zakia, five. The three boys are younger: Shaib is seven; Shekeb and Fawad, about five.

Imitating the teachers of my childhood, I always begin in the same way: "Did you do your study exercises at home? Whoever didn't do his or her exercises, sit to one side; we'll see about that later. Now, today we're going to discuss the importance of water on Earth and in human life. What is water for?"

I can see myself back in class, listening to my teacher. Mama enrolled me in the school in Mikrorayan 1, on the south bank of the Kabul River, and that's where I completed my primary education. My father would drop me off at eight, and Shakila picked me up at eleven-thirty.

In my class there was a girl named Wahida. She was from Kandahar, the big city at the edge of the Rigistan Desert, and since she was older than the rest of us, the teacher made her the head of the class, an honor that should have been mine since I had the best grades. I envied her and thought she was too bossy. When Wahida announced that she was going back to Kandahar, she must have expected that I would be sad, but on the contrary, I remember telling her, "It's much better for you to go back there." I became head of the class with proud isfaction. Now that I think about it, I wasn't very nice at the time.

All through primary school we wore traditional clothing, but when we began high school, we had to wear a uniform: a brown dress over white overalls. The Soviets had just constructed a modern building in Mikrorayan that they called the Friendship School. Within the next six months, they built two more. Since school was now compulsory, they took certain measures to encourage families to send their children to class. They granted an allowance of 1,500 afghanis per pupil per month, and in the high schools they provided free blue dresses for the girls, free gray shirts for everyone. This system lasted only six months. We called it *emdad,* or "disco-aid," because the disco style of the eighties was synonymous to us with the luxuries we received from the Soviets.

When the army withdrew in 1989, the Soviets left behind a certain number of "advisers" in all areas, whom we immediately dubbed "the ones who missed the last truck out." There were many Soviet instructors in our school during the occupation, but in 1989 there were only two left, one of whom was in my class. Farhad, a classmate who was very sure of himself, used to tease him regularly by throwing wads of paper at his head.

"Why do you stay here when everyone else has left?" he'd call out.

Since Farhad's father was an important member of

the new faction in power, no one dared reprimand him. I thought he was rather rude. After a while, these two instructors must have left as well, although I don't think Farhad's paper wads had anything to do with it. But his hatred of the Soviets was understandable.

In our neighborhood, many children had lost their fathers who had gone missing or died in prison during those years: my playmates Fereshta, Yama, Aymal, and Babrak, and especially Anita, who made my heart bleed. Anita and I were in the same class nine years in a row. I liked her a lot. She was a thin girl with white skin and chestnut hair, winsome and gay. When I learned she'd lost her father, I drew even closer to her. Under the Soviets her father had been arrested and imprisoned, and had vanished without a trace. Her mother never managed to find out why he had been arrested or where he had been taken—probably to Pol-i-Sharkhi, like my brother Wahid. But unlike thousands of other men, Anita's father never came back. The only memento Anita has of him is a photo showing her as a little girl in his arms. Her mother cried when she showed it to me. Anita reacted differently to this loss: She lived on the surface of things, a dreamy soul who loved to take part in theatricals at school and sometimes sang for the class. It was her way of surviving and hoping. She would often say to me, "He'll come back some day."

Compared to her, I was blessed: My parents were

alive and I knew their whole story, thanks to one of my aunts, who never tired of telling it. They had married for love, when Mama was a student in medicine attending free courses given by German doctors at the Goethe Institut in Kabul. At that time she was doing her supervisory period as a nurse at Mastourat Hospital, which is where my father met and fell in love with her. For four years, she never noticed, while he was sending her poems and doing his best to be charming and attentive to this *belle indifférente*. She had simply noticed his kindness, and it was one of her fellow nurses who opened her eyes.

When Mama returned his love, those around her opposed the marriage, as did Papa's grandmother, who was afraid to bring into the family "a woman who had a university education, who worked in a hospital, and who might not show enough respect" to the old lady.

Finally, Papa told my mother: "If they keep trying to prevent our marriage, well, then—I'll kidnap you!"

So they won their case and had a lovely engagement. Papa took his fiancée to the movies, on walks, to restaurants. One of Mama's girlfriends, who worked for the police, once remarked to her: "Alia, you picked a man, a real one! The proof is that he's not afraid to take you to a restaurant." At the time, my aunt explained, a man did not take a respectable woman to restaurants.

My parents were married in 1964, and my brothers and sisters and I are all proud to be the children of a marriage like theirs. That's how our family history began, and in a way it's a symbol of Afghanistan. Papa is a Pashtun, and Mama is a Tajik, and they've stayed together, just as our country has in the face of wars and fratricidal ethnic strife.

One morning in the middle of winter in 1999, one of my students passes on a request from his parents that I explain the war against the British. The parents often ask me to teach certain subjects.

Given the boy's age, I have to keep my explanation simple.

"The British tried to invade our country, but Afghans don't like foreign invaders. So, even though the British had sophisticated weapons while our people only had sticks, they fought back courageously. They won, the British left, and they never came back again! The British didn't know anything about our way of life. I'll give you an example. They had observed that Afghans would often take from their pockets and chew some dusty little balls that looked like tiny clumps of dirt. The British were intrigued and wondered what they were for."

"What were they, Latifa?"

"In the countryside, people gather mulberries, dry them, grind them up, and make this powder into an edible paste that's very sweet and lasts a long time. It's called *talkhan* and it gives new energy to men during battles.

"After their defeat by the Afghans, the British didn't carry off any precious *talkhan.* They took gold, jewelry, and many ancient objects they admired. But since they couldn't manage to transport these treasures across the mountains, they hid them here and there along the path they took to go home. And some people say they still dream of coming back one day to get them."

Another day, another question.

"My father says that King Habibullah Khan never did anything good for our country, unlike President Daoud. He wants to know what you think."

"We'll talk about that tomorrow."

The question has taken me by surprise; afraid of bungling my answer because the names and dates are a little mixed up in my memory, I prefer to ask my family to explain that period of our history to me later this evening.

So the next morning, well informed on the subject, I can tell my pupil that his father is right.

"King Habibullah Khan did not serve his country well. In his palace he had three hundred women all for his own pleasure! His son Amanullah Khan declared independence and drove the British from our soil, but President Daoud had other ambitions: He wanted to develop Afghanistan into a modern state. For example, he envisioned that we would be able to manufacture cars and all sorts of similar products. That's why he didn't want to be king, but president of a republic. Unfortunately, he did not have time to achieve his goals, because the Soviets intervened."

When I was in school, our history courses began with the Anglo-Afghan Wars. Then came the "modern" period that my parents lived through, with the reign of Mohammed Zahir Shah, followed by the government of his cousin Daoud.

I remember that my history teacher in high school, who was explaining the nineteenth-century Anglo-Afghan Wars to us, tried to make a comparison and got so carried away that he made a curious slip of the tongue, "The Soviets left Afghanistan in 1878, like the British in 1989. Uh . . . no . . . I mean, they left in the same way—retreating in defeat!"

I recall in particular the winter of 1988–1989. The Soviets were about to leave the country. Kabul was in the grip of the coldest temperatures in living memory. Food supplies were almost exhausted. The mujahideen had surrounded and blockaded the capital, and we were running out of everything. My sister and I would line up separately in front of two different bakeries to buy six loaves of bread. It was the same with gas, because the electric towers had been destroyed by the resistance, so everyone was using gas rings for cooking and coal for heat. Lines were growing longer all over the city. It took half a day to get the least little item. Some people started waiting in midafternoon and reached the head of the line at around seven o'clock; others arrived at the stores well before dawn, sometimes at three in the morning, in the hope of getting their turn at nine. These hardships lasted for four months, and people actually dropped dead standing in line. When there wasn't any bread, the wealthier Kabulis ate cake—while we were supposedly in the midst of a revolution! I ate so much cake I got sick of it.

The Soviet planes resupplying the city landed only at night, and the newspapers spoke of "Kabul on life support." With the rocket fire, the endless lines, the price of rice, sugar, and flour, people in the city were nervous wrecks: The slightest thing would set them off and start them fighting among themselves. Many seriously considered leaving Kabul.

Some married their daughters to boys who lived in the West, planning to join their daughters later and lead the entire family into exile. Others tried to sell their possessions to finance an often secret trip abroad. Kabul had lost even the artificial joy it had known under the Soviets.

Finally, in the spring of 1989, the radio announced that our reserve stocks had been replenished: There would be no more problems with provisions. Strangely enough, Kabulis knew almost nothing about what was happening out in the countryside. Television offered us lots of entertainment programs, as if to hypnotize us: concerts, the Miss Kabul or Miss Afghanistan pageant, Indian films. Theaters were open; radio stations poured out floods of music. Now and then we did notice that there seemed to be more people in the city streets, but we knew nothing about the families that had fled their homes and villages during the fighting between government troops and the resistance forces. The population of the capital was slowly swelling before our thoughtless eyes. We didn't want to face reality. Of course the mujahideen existed, of course we knew about the resistance, but I believe we were still hoping that the situation would resolve itself, the country would be reunited, and peace would return.

Then came Jalalabad. During the summer of 1991, two years after the Soviet retreat, the mujahideen began a great battle to take that city with the massive support of the Pakistani army. The Afghan army and the Communist government mobilized the population. It was on that occasion that Dr. Najibullah gave his famous speech on Aryana Square. The authorities aimed to defend Jalalabad against the mujahideen onslaught, but above all to fight Pakistani interference. Women were recruited to provide security in the capital. That was the first time I saw women in military uniform: They were everywhere, at intersections and on the main avenues. They worked at Kabul's grain storage and milling facilities, which stayed open around the clock to ensure adequate supplies of bread. They drove the electric public buses. They worked in administration, in banks; they sang on television. Girls in the Communist Youth League made the rounds of the schools to collect donations for the army. This mobilization even inspired young amateur singers to give charity concerts for the glory of the armed forces. And so you saw kids imitating Madonna or Michael Jackson singing for the Afghan army. Still, I certainly knew about the girls in my neighborhood who were upset because their fiancés were leaving for the front.

The day before the mujahideen arrived, at the end of April 1992, we were attending a marriage in the Hotel Kabul in the center of town, across from the main bank and not far from the presidential palace and the treasury. The festivities got under way at around four o'clock. Girls and boys were dancing in Western dress, and we dined before the religious ceremony was scheduled to begin. Suddenly a soldier rushed into the room and explained to the father of the bride that resistance units had entered the capital, and that the wedding ceremony should be completed quickly. Since most of the women were in low-cut dresses, they hastily put on their husbands' suit jackets, and everyone rushed home.

Five minutes later, it was all over. The young groom's older brother took my sisters and me straight to our apartment, where our parents were surprised to see us back so early. They hadn't expected us until after midnight.

Shakila asked if the radio had announced anything, but there had been no news bulletins. The next morning, things still seemed normal, and we all behaved as usual.

At around eleven, Shakila came to get me at school, telling the teacher simply that I was needed at home.

"There could be war in Kabul," she explained to me on the way back, "and I have to warn the others. I'll call Papa at the store."

I heard her ask him to buy some provisions and come home as fast as possible. Then she called the airport to tell Soraya to come home, too. Shakila was trying to stay calm, but every five minutes she would go to the window to see if our parents were coming. An hour and a half later, everyone had returned.

"Why all this hurry?" asked Papa.

"I was on my way to work at the newspaper as usual and started noticing that stores were closed and that people were constructing barricades out of sandbags. The armed men I saw were wearing turbans. Well, no one besides the military has the right to carry weapons inside the city! When our taxi got as far as the Electric Power and Water Ministry, not far from Festival Square, a soldier waved us to a halt. I showed him my press pass and explained that I was going to the newspaper offices, but he told me that Gulbuddin Hekmatyar's men were there and that I should turn around. When I asked him who this Hekmatyar was, a man in traditional clothes, wearing a turban and a beard, shouted: 'We are the Hizb-i-Islami of Hekmatyar!'

"And suddenly the taxi was surrounded by all these men in turbans, so I told the driver to turn around immediately. The driver was maneuvering the car to get out of there when the soldier who'd stopped me signaled again—he wanted me to take along two young women who worked at the ministry. They told me that these bearded men had hit and humiliated them because they were wearing skirts and pantyhose, that the men had torn off their pantyhose and tied them around their necks, spitting in their faces and calling them Communists! After we got across the bridge to get back to our neighborhood, everything was quiet. No one could believe that the situation was so different only a few hundred yards away."

That evening we had supper at around seven-thirty, and it wasn't long before fighting broke out in the city. Shakila rushed up to Saber's apartment on the sixth floor to find out where the battles were. Even though it was illegal to own binoculars at the time, Saber had a pair. He was in love with Victoria, a girl who lived in the building across the way, and somehow he'd gotten his hands on these binoculars so that he could watch his girlfriend from his balcony. Saber's mother worked in the janitorial staff at the presidential palace, and she told Shakila that bearded men had sent all the women there home that day, accusing them of being Communists.

So Hekmatyar's men were already at the presidential palace. From the sixth floor, Shakila saw the glow of combat in front of the palace, in the area of Pole Mahmoud Khan, as well as over by the hospital and the neighborhood of Shashdarak, near the radio and television building. Yet the radio was broadcasting normally, except that no one was giving any news about the fighting.

Shakila was still quite shaken, and kept repeating, "You see! I was right, I was right."

Soraya and I had piled some cushions in front of our bedroom window, and I thought about what the girls at school had been saying lately: "If the extremists get to Kabul, we won't be able to wear makeup anymore, or Western clothes. Just wait—they'll even forbid us to ride bicycles!"

A few minutes later, the explosions came so close that the tenants on the fifth and sixth floors, who were most at risk from the rockets, went downstairs to the basement.

The fighting continued for more than two days without us receiving any information from the government. Finally, on the third day, Radio Kabul announced that the men of Hekmatyar's faction had been driven out and their attempt to take over the city foiled.

Commander Massoud was now the master of Kabul,

and his government, the Islamic State of Afghanistan, issued a declaration of its new constitution. I still remember the welcome words we heard that day: "As of next Saturday, everyone, women in particular, must return to work. Both the girls' and the boys' schools will be reopened."

My classmates were just as relieved as I was. Hekmatyar frightened us so much that the only "politics" we followed in those days, we girls who wanted the freedom to learn and thus to work, was that this fanatic should be driven as far away as possible, up into the north or out into Pakistan.

A week later, there was a television report on the crimes committed by the Communists. Groups of prisoners were shown; executed en masse at Pol-i-Sharkhi; hundreds of pairs of shoes lying scattered about; and mass graves. When the Communists were in power, thousands of people accused of anti-Communism had been arrested, executed, and thrown into common graves. There were rumors about Afghan political prisoners who'd been sent to Siberia. A few months later, my friend Anita came to see me to say goodbye, happy and full of hope: She was leaving with her mother for the U.S.S.R. to look for her father, and they'd sold their house to pay for the trip. I was just so sad to see them go off in search of a ghost.

Anita eventually returned from the U.S.S.R. She never found her father.

The atmosphere in Kabul was now rather bizarre: We were still free to move around, study, work, yet at the same time we had to endure the daily war that Hekmatyar and his men forced upon us by besieging the city.

In 1993, the fighting became horrific in its violence and intensity. Afghans don't go to school in the winter because it's too cold, and schools became refuges for displaced families. Neighborhoods in the south, west, and downtown area of the city were particularly hard hit. Kabulis were fleeing to the northern neighborhoods, while some were leaving for Jalalabad or Pakistan. It was a real ethnic war. Pashtuns were killing Hazaras, Hazaras were killing Tajiks. The man most responsible for this butchery was still Gulbuddin Hekmatyar, who everyone knew was completely dependent on the Pakistani intelligence service.

To spread terror in the city, mysterious gangs of boys poisoned food by injecting a toxic substance into fruits and vegetables. Some people became ill, and a certain number even died. The inhabitants of Kabul were so afraid that they no longer dared to buy fresh produce from street vendors. After a few weeks, one of these gangs was arrested and shown on television, and the food scare subsided.

Rockets fell absolutely anyplace. On some days, there were three hundred of them, or even a thousand.

The hospitals were full of wounded. Medicines were in short supply. Doctors worked night and day.

In January 1994, in alliance with the troops of General Dostum and the Hazara commander Mazari, Hekmatyar's forces started a bloody campaign.

At 4 A.M. on January 1, bombardments began that continued without letup for one week, which we spent in the basement with our neighbors. Electricity and running water were cut throughout the city. Then the combatants decided on a sort of truce that allowed foreign diplomats to leave the capital. We took advantage of the lull as well, to take refuge in the northern sector of the city, and we saw that thousands of people, entire families, had been forced to abandon their homes. This battle lasted for more than seven months, burning and blasting much of Kabul into rubble. The university, one of the largest in the region: burned. The university library, the second most important in Asia: pillaged and burned. The museum: looted and destroyed. And in spite of everything we went on living. I kept going to school, and Shakila got married on a day when three hundred rockets fell on Kabul.

Having lived through so much war, we had become indifferent to the tragedy of our country, so anesthetized that we were blind to the final threat that still lay in wait for us: a secret movement of religious students, a new militia that would take advantage of the tribal infighting over Kabul and seize a third of the country in the southwest at the end of 1994.

We had a little more than two years left to make the most of that strange freedom in a city under perpetual siege. I was fourteen, the same age as little Ramika, who takes off her *chadri* as she enters my bedroom to sit quietly on the floor and listen to me read a poem by Mohammed Hafez Shirazi.

To me the world was a house
Where I searched for knowledge everywhere
I loved to wander under many skies
Gathering up each nuance of thought
In diverse fruits that furnish
The nourishment of my philosophy.

Ramika will write it down at my dictation and recite it to me later on.

She's of an age that allows the Taliban to enforce the monstrous decree announced as soon as they seized power: "All girls must be married." Not long ago, I think it was last year, a woman knocked on the door of an apartment in a building near ours. She was a decoy, a procuress who ferrets out young Afghan girls for the Taliban. Alone at home with her three daughters, the woman in the apartment opened the door, only to be rushed by some *talibs* who beat her unconscious and kidnapped her daughters. The decoy claimed to the neighbors that the girls were already married to her sons, and that she had the right to make "her" daughters-in-law live in her home.

Since that episode, it's either my father or Daoud who opens the door to strangers.

One of my girl cousins was caught in this diabolical trap. A *talib* was so determined to have her, so threatening and tenacious, that she was obliged to marry another boy, much younger than she was, even though she had stubbornly refused to get married until then.

There are so many, many stories like that, shocking or simply deplorable stories of the shattered lives of girls my age or as young as Ramika. Tonight, I'm going to pray for the impossible: the return of freedom for women, and I'll be especially vigilant when I watch from the window as Ramika's *chadri* disappears down the street.

I've changed.

I've grown up.

SIX

Kite Hunting

Papa has been worrying about the risk we've been running ever since we opened our underground school. He doesn't talk about it because he can see that it's a welcome distraction for Soraya, Daoud, and me, and even Mama has perked up a bit, but Papa often thinks back sadly to the way things used to be.

"Ah, I remember when you were going to school, when I would take you to your English lessons. Now I watch you hiding like a thief to teach these children who will never have what you did. Things were already hard for you, but now . . ."

My poor father seems to bear the weight of the world on his shoulders.

Life in the apartment has been more lively ever since our pupils began coming here every day. My mother helps out; at first we tried not to disturb her too much, but now she pitches in as much as she can. She cooks for the children at noon and is pleased to see them eat. When they leave, she encourages them.

"Well done! This is a way to keep up the good fight."

This change in our routine has led to visits from our women neighbors, because their children are in our home. Before, they only came to see Mama for health reasons, and their visits became less frequent as they grew more afraid. Then they stopped coming altogether, because Mama ran out of medical supplies and couldn't treat them anymore. Now Mama can safely welcome them again, for these women can hardly denounce a secret school attended by their own children. And these kids are in such danger! The girls most of all, but the boys as well. There's a horrific rumor going around the city. They say little boys have disappeared, and some of them have been found mutilated or dead. The Taliban are supposedly using them for organ trafficking. "They say." There's lots of "they say" in Kabul. If only we had an independent newspaper at least, as we did when Shakila worked in the capital; she could have carried out an investigation. But I'm dreaming: The city is locked up tight, a citadel of silence. All we hear are whispers, hearsay, reports that can never be verified.

Before the Taliban, I'd taken a training course at Shakila's newspaper, and when I was thirteen some friends and I decided to publish our review, *Dawn*. There wasn't anything out there at the time that was geared to us, and we wanted to fill this niche. With Shakila's help, Farida, Maryam, Saber, and I published our creation at home: It appeared every trimester. Handwritten in a single edition, this one copy made the rounds of the school, our friends, and our friends' families.

On the last page we'd glue an envelope for our readers' suggestions, which allowed us to focus the next edition on subjects our readers and friends found especially interesting.

We'd take articles on women's issues from Iranian magazines and collect information about different university departments and career possibilities. Lighter articles were devoted to fashion, makeup, music. I cut out pictures of models or celebrities and pasted them in. We talked about the latest books, new CDs. I photocopied postcards of American or Indian movie stars and wrote up anecdotes about their lives. And for more serious topics, I got help on our political and general news pages from my sisters, especially Shakila.

When the Taliban arrived, I'd been about to wrap up the last number of the year, which I never finished. I just didn't have the heart. Farida and Daoud took over, which for my brother was a way of trying to keep me interested in our review. He would have liked me to carry on, but I really didn't want to anymore. I abandoned it, and the others did too. Where can we get news when the media are censored? We're completely cut off from the world. Aside from a few messages from Wahid in Russia; the rare letters Daoud receives from his pals in exile in London, Germany, or Holland; and the evening radio broadcasts we listen to in secret, we hear nothing. This void is completely disorienting. Daoud claims that Kabul no longer exists for the outside world. And his buddies abroad think that there are no more Afghans left in the capital, just Pakistanis.

Whenever Soraya, Daoud, and I talk together about what people in the rest of the world think, Daoud is the most pessimistic.

"You think they're concerned? I don't. They don't even know where Afghanistan is. And I bet they don't believe what's happening to us. It's got nothing to do with them. Even Afghans living abroad couldn't care less!"

Twice we've been lucky enough to receive magazines from the Arab Emirates through a friend of Daoud's who works for Aryana. The airline company is still operating, but without women, and its only destinations are Islamabad, Dubai, and Jedda, in Saudi Arabia. Two magazines in three years; that's not much in the way of fresh information.

Farida has a talent for answering her own questions, and she's the one who wakes us all up.

"How about if we publish our review again? Don't you want to? I do! All we have to do is get started."

She offers to go walking around the city, an invisible reporter under her *chadri*, collecting news items for the next issue. Daoud will help by obtaining paper supplies, and since he has beautiful handwriting, he'll be in charge of the calligraphy.

We'll miss Shakila. Since she got married, we all miss her smile and her authority. It was she who supervised our studies, and she kept a close eye on both Soraya and me. It was thanks to her that Papa took us to the movies, because she loved music and films. Shakila was an excellent student, curious about everything. When she was eleven she received the best grade in her Russian class, which earned her an invitation to visit the U.S.S.R.—and the fulminations of Wahid, who refused to let her go. But she stood her ground.

My sister began working for an independent newspaper while she was still at the university. I remember how delighted I was to be a trainee at her paper. I was thirteen, and I went off to work with her in spite of the rockets crashing down on us, beginning the destruction of Kabul. In 1994, we were only just starting to understand the complexity of the quarrels among the various resistance factions. Take the abortive coup d'état of January 1, for example, when the Uzbek militia of General Dostum and Hekmatyar's ultra-fundamentalists tried to overthrow

President Rabbani, a Tajik supported by the forces of Ahmed Shah Massoud. Reporters baptized this episode "the fifth battle of Kabul." A million people took to the roads, fleeing the fighting around the city. The coup d'état failed, and Massoud drove the fundamentalists out of the capital in June, but Shakila said we would never have peace.

"Pakistan does not want to see a strong government come out of a solid alliance among the mujahideen. It wants us disunited, and as long as our country is destabilized by tribal wars, Pakistan can quietly continue its aggressive attitude toward India while enjoying the support of the United States. American foreign policy in Asia is a dreadful mistake."

One morning, we arrived at the paper to learn tragic news. Mirwais Jalil, an Afghan journalist working for the BBC, had just been murdered by Gulbuddin Hekmatyar. That afternoon we went to the hospital to see his body, which bore clear signs of the vicious torture the poor man had endured. A foreign reporter who'd been with him revealed the reason he had been executed: Jalil had filmed Arabs and Pakistanis fighting for Hekmatyar, who had wanted to intimidate us and destroy proof that foreigners had joined the ranks of Afghan extremists.

Every evening Shakila reported to us what she'd heard at work or at the university, and she wrote everything down in a notebook. I listened to her eagerly and used certain stories in our own little review. I remember perfectly the "case" of Mrs. Zarmina, for example, which clearly demonstrates the fiendish machinations of the Communist administration.

At the end of the 1980s, Mrs. Zarmina was a cleaning woman at Riassat Melli Bus, the Department of Public Transportation for the city of Kabul. She was a good soul, illiterate, who had joined the Communist Party at her workplace, which was no doubt a requirement for her job. To join the party, she had to swear never to lie to her superiors and never to betray the party. Well, one day while she's busy cleaning an office, she overhears a conversation among the director of the department, his assistant, and a few other officials. She realizes that these men are discussing the resale of bus parts, which is absolutely illegal. The director asks his assistant to arrange for city buses to break down more often and be withdrawn from service so that they can be sent to the wrecker.

"We'll sell the motors and chassis parts and split the money ourselves."

Having promised never to lie to the party, Mrs. Zarmina faithfully reports what she's heard to the administrative offices of the Department of Public Transportation. Present at the time are Farid Mazdak, a political watchdog, and the deputy of the Watan Party, which was then in power. The wretched Mrs. Zarmina is of course unaware that she is dealing with an organized mafia.

Farid Mazdak bestows upon her the Medal of Merit and the grateful thanks of the party.

The next evening, when Mrs. Zarmina fails to return home after work, her worried husband shows up at Riassat Melli Bus, where no one has any idea where she might be. After a week, her husband returns to the company with his children and demands to see his wife. By now he has learned the whole story and suspects that she is somewhere in the building.

And in fact the director has been holding her prisoner on the premises throughout the week. He summons the husband to his office, locks the door behind him, and forces him to watch as his wife is raped. After which, the director tells the poor man that if he's not happy, all he has to do is divorce his wife. He then tries to make the husband sign a petition for divorce. Completely at his wit's end, the husband doesn't know what to do. So the director has Mrs. Zarmina's head shaved as her children look on. When the husband still refuses to sign, the infuriated director has the children thrown into the Kabul River, which is right in front of the Riassat Melli Bus Company building. Mrs. Zarmina manages to escape her captors and jumps into the river, saving her son, but the current sweeps her daughter away to her death.

Crazed with anguish, the desperate woman goes home, only to find that her husband wants nothing more to do with her. She doesn't give up, she intends to fight to the bitter end, so she goes to make a complaint at the Ministry of Transportation. However, General Khalil, who is also implicated in this black marketeering, orders his bodyguards to beat her and throw her out.

The tragedy of Mrs. Zarmina goes on for more than two years. Everyone thinks she's a madwoman, nobody believes her story, and even when she sends a petition to Fazal Haq Khaliqyar, the non-Communist prime minister in Dr. Najibullah's government, he refuses to grant her an interview.

Shakila writes an account of this business in her paper, which is still—fortunately—an independent publication in spite of threats from the Watan Party. And this enables Mrs. Zarmina to triumph at last over injustice. When the resistance takes possession of the capital in April 1992, the poor woman demands redress from the new masters of Kabul. The crooks are finally arrested and imprisoned. But when the Taliban arrive, Mrs. Zarmina loses the right to work and has to flee to Pakistan, where she and her son are living, according to the last news Shakila had of her, in the refugee camp at Nasser Bagh, a mile or so outside Peshawar.

Stories of rape were common in the newspapers of that period, and they are still common under the Taliban—but not in the papers. Under the Communist regime, Kamela Habib, a reporter on the weekly *Saba'won*, published an article about a case while taking the precaution of changing the names of those involved, since influential party members were implicated in the affair.

Parwin was a young woman who worked in the Ministry of Education. The rapists invited her to a party; when she arrived, she saw that she was the only woman, but it was too late for her to leave on her own. They plied her with liquor and carried out their plan. There were a lot of them—even the driver joined the gang rape. The house watchman dropped her off at the hospital, unconscious. Kamela Habib happened to be at the hospital, and Parwin was able to tell her everything before she died.

Another unforgettable story that made the rounds of the newspaper offices concerned a monstrous child born at the Malalai Maternity Hospital in Kabul. The baby, who lived for only eight hours, had a hideous face: a single eye in the center of its forehead, one ear almost on top of its head, its mouth over in the left cheek. It had neither arms nor legs. Some doctors claimed the deformities were the result of stress from the war during the mother's pregnancy! After lab tests, however, they finally agreed that mother and child had been exposed to chemical substances carried by Scud missiles, which Soviet troops had used for the first time in the Salang Valley. The baby's mother was from Salang.

That story goes back to a time when despite the civil war, we weren't condemned to a single source of information, a time when we had television, when newspapers were published, when life was still possible. Most of what we've heard lately on Radio Sharia still—as always—concerns women: They are forbidden to speak in public, as the sound of their voices might "provoke" the merchants of the bazaar. We still have our "street radio," whispered by those who come and go freely: men. The flood of "they say" swirling through Kabul is once again tossing around news of bin Laden, the Taliban's Saudi friend, as well as of the marriage ("they" don't know where or when) of Mullah Omar, the Taliban leader, to one of bin Laden's many daughters. We hear this wedding was so sumptuously depraved that it seems the Taliban don't bother to live by their own rules.

Far removed from such luxury, one of my former classmates, Hafeza, came to our apartment and offered to rent us books for 500 afghanis per volume. Her mother bakes bread for a few coins, like many destitute women. We felt so bad for her that Daoud decided to rent one book a week, even if we don't necessarily read it. Daoud is a quiet one, and tender hearted, the opposite of our oldest brother. Daoud doesn't say much, but he's always ready to help.

In July 1998, he got married. Ordinarily, a wedding is a huge celebration. Daoud's left us with cloudy, bitter memories. I feel as if it never happened, almost as if he weren't actually married, and yet his wife, Marie, lives with us, according to our custom.

Daoud really wanted to get married. One day, a friend of his spoke to him about Marie, one of his young wife's friends, a girl from a good family whom he thought might be a fine match for Daoud. He invited Daoud to his home, and since Marie lived in the house next door, at least my brother was able to catch a glimpse of her in her parents' garden, even though he wasn't able to meet her the way young people used to meet before the Taliban. It was frustrating for Daoud, obviously, but he'd liked what he'd seen, and in any case, he was now twenty-nine years old and had made up his mind to get married.

So my parents made their request in the proper fashion. In Afghanistan, it's always the parents who organize marriages; my grandmother used to say that love comes after the *nikha*, the religious ceremony. There was no engagement, given the situation in Kabul, and we were sad that the future couple couldn't see each other. No celebration, no music, no presents, no lovely gown . . . Mama often used to tell us that for her wedding she had worn a magnificent green dress created by the official tailor of the royal court, Mr. Azar. Then, for the evening reception, she wore a long white dress from Paris lent to her by the wife of the head of the king's intelligence service. Green is the color of hope and of Islam, and the green dress is traditional attire for the religious ceremony. In the evening, the atmosphere is more Western, and the white dress is a European influence. During the wedding vows, the bride and groom exchange rings, and a respectable elderly lady of the family places henna in the palms of their hands. Then the couple look at themselves in a special mirror they will later take into their bedroom. The newlyweds read a verse from the Koran and share a sweet drink so that their union will be sweet for as long as they live. At the end of the ceremony, a sheep is slaughtered, and if the blood splashes onto the bride's shoes, it means she'll always be faithful to her husband.

None of that for Daoud and Marie. Well, we decided that somehow we had to try to make the wedding a festive occasion.

But where could we go? It was impossible to have a party in a restaurant, the way we'd done to entertain a hundred guests for Shakila's wedding. No establishment would host a mixed gathering of men and women anymore. And our apartment is too small, too exposed to the curiosity of neighbors and the Taliban. Unless we hid down in a basement, as we did during the worst of the rocket bombardments, we didn't know how we could celebrate this marriage.

Marie's parents lived in a house with a garden in another neighborhood of Kabul, and since their neighbors were on good terms with Daoud's friend, we took the risk of gathering at their home for the ceremony.

It had been a long time since Soraya and I had set foot outside our home, and a long time since we had last attended a wedding. But there were no preparations, none of the excitement of wearing makeup or buying material for pretty new dresses. That was out of the question. The guests were reduced to the bare minimum: a few of Daoud's friends and the members of both families. My brother was depressed and disappointed at not being able to wear a nice suit and tie, which are forbidden. His chums were making fun of him.

"It's no big deal. Anyway, there won't be any photographs either, because they're forbidden, too. Nobody will know you weren't wearing a suit!"

Then, seeing how sad Daoud was, one of his friends couldn't take it anymore.

"No, it's not right, I'm not going to marry off my pal without at least videotaping it. He has to have a souvenir. I'll take care of it."

So he came with his video camera. We started out doing things according to Taliban rules, which forbid mixed company, even for a wedding. The women were in one room, the men in another. For the ceremony, though, the couple had to be together, after all, to exchange their rings. The families gathered in the garden. Daoud and Marie were standing near each other. It was the most symbolic moment, so Daoud's friend got out his camera, another friend put a music tape into a cassette player.

Suddenly someone shouted: "The Taliban! They're coming!"

Instant panic. The tapes and cassette player vanished within a minute—nobody could figure out how the guy did it. But the Taliban had heard music! Furious, they looked everywhere, with no luck. Our amateur cameraman, however, who hadn't had time to stash his video camera, was caught in the act. The intruders took their revenge on the poor man and beat him up. They grabbed his camera, trampled it in a rage as though it were the devil's own invention, and destroyed the only pictures of Daoud's wedding.

While the Taliban were savoring the effect of their performance, our few guests slipped away. We drove home with the bride, hurrying off like thieves instead of enjoying the traditional festive departure of the newlyweds. It was heartbreaking.

My brother's friend was not seriously injured, thank goodness, but he had lost his camera and everyone was upset: Papa infuriated, Soraya in tears, and Daoud perfectly miserable. He was so ashamed to be bringing home his bride like that! The welcoming of a new member into the family is a joyous occasion, and the wedding of a son is usually celebrated much more elaborately. When a daughter leaves, it's not the same thing, the happiness is for her husband's family. Poor Daoud, cheated of that happiness, humiliated by two or three *talibs* trying to show off their authority. Sometimes I wonder why these brutes deprive an entire population of parties and games, and family memories, and the answer is always chillingly simple: They want to rob us of life. To exterminate us, slowly but surely, for their own benefit.

There are no more kites in the skies of Kabul. There used to be dozens of them whirling over the city. Boys clambered across the rooftops to catch the wind, risking falls as they gazed up in the air. And they fell often. Every year boys injured while flying kites would wind up in the hospital. Still, their rainbow-colored paper birds were an emblem of our sky.

Children without enough money to buy kites made *chelaks*, formidable kite-catchers made of a small stone attached to a string. These kids preyed on the kites of others, throwing their *chelaks* over the lines of the kites they coveted. If their aim was true, the two strings would tangle, and the junior thieves had only to drag their booty down to the ground and seize it. Kite hunting provoked fights, especially since some hunters used a modified *chelak*, equipped with two stones, which made the hunt even more dangerous. The *chelak* wasn't just used by little thieves; it was also a game played by those who, like Daoud, couldn't manage to handle their own kites.

Once when Soraya was trying to cheer me up, she told me the story of the kite that fell on top of Daoud when he was little.

"It was in our old home, the one before we lived here, and you weren't born yet. Daoud was playing with his *chelak* out in the garden, and wham—the *chelak* of a boy next door that had missed its mark landed right on his head. He didn't dare come home because his mouth was bleeding, and he was afraid of being scolded. One of his playmates, Abdullah, lived on the ground floor of the building, and his mother was a nurse, so Abdullah took Daoud inside to see his mama. She put a stitch in Daoud's cut and brought him upstairs to us. But an hour later, it was Abdullah who was hurt, falling from the roof with his kite. His knee was bleeding and his mother came to Mama in tears to tell her he was wounded. This time it was Mama who had to do the stitching up and bandaging!"

Daoud hardly ever got into fights; he was a quiet boy, a studious child who received good grades, especially in math. He was a devoted movie fan and had a fine collection of miniature cars, to which he added a new one every month.

Mama still tells us about the day her sons were circumcised, both at the same time. There was a great celebration, with more than a hundred guests. She had had white suits made for the boys, a huge sheep had been slaughtered, and garlands of electric lights festooned the courtyard. Circumcision is usually performed here by a barber or a doctor, and of course Mama had chosen a doctor. My father had carefully explained to his sons what was going to happen. Wahid went through his ordeal with no problem, but Daoud was quite frightened, and when his turn came, the doctor gave him the usual kind of advice: "Look up at the sky and the birds, young man . . ."

Knowing what was coming and rigid with apprehension, Daoud shot back, "Just go ahead and cut! I know what you're up to."

Whenever Mama and our aunts told that story, Wahid and Daoud would grumble in exasperation that it certainly hadn't been a treat for them, to see others celebrating while they were in pain.

Wahid was a scrapper and enlisted in the army, whereas Daoud tried to avoid the army at all costs. In the winter of 1987, Daoud was eighteen and had just passed his final exams at Omar Shahid High School. He went out one morning to check on the exam results, but when he hadn't returned home by nightfall, the whole family was worried. Papa went around the neighborhood to ask if any of his friends had seen him, and Shakila called Wahid at his barracks. Wahid told her to sit tight, he would look into it. A military truck pulled up in front of our building at around midnight. Wahid got out, in uniform, followed by a very shaken Daoud.

I didn't see what happened—I was too young—but my sisters have told me the story so many times that I remember it just as if I'd been there.

Wahid lectured Daoud, ordering him not to leave the

house anymore, and returned to his barracks. Then Daoud told us the rest.

"They instructed us to wait in front of the school for the exam results, and after two hours they brought us into the courtyard. All of a sudden soldiers surrounded the buildings. Some officers came into the courtyard and turned the first classroom into a recruitment station, telling us they would call students' names in alphabetical order so they could be assigned to different army units. I and my whole class were posted to Gardez, in the south! Kids with connections started phoning and within the hour they were heading home, but my pals and I had no idea what to do or whom to call. Everyone was scared of ending up on the front with a Kalashnikov, like Wahid. They weren't supposed to be drafting us because we haven't finished our studies—they grant exemptions for going to college. Anyway, that's when I saw Wahid arrive in his presidential guard uniform, with six soldiers behind him, and he was mad. The soldiers with us saluted, he sent them to get the school principal right away, and told him, 'This is illegal; you have no right to keep the students here without informing their parents.' The chief recruiting officer said that he was just following orders. Wahid radioed the army enlistment center to speak to the staff on duty at the garrison and was told that the students should, in fact, be released. All my pals took off, and Wahid brought me home."

This happened during the period when the Soviets were looking for young men to conscript into the Afghan army. Some, like my eldest brother, had freely chosen to enlist, since he had to do his military service sooner or later, but Daoud was only eighteen, and Wahid absolutely did not want his brother to lead the same life he did. He knew perfectly well that Daoud hated the army and the war, and that he could never cope with fighting the Afghan resistance in a Soviet-led battalion.

Daoud hid at home for three months while he waited for the university entrance exam. During that time Shakila had to do the shopping and errands in his place. She would take me along every day to rent videos because we had to take his mind off his troubles and, above all, prevent him from going out. This wasn't easy, because he was rattling around in the apartment like a bear in a cage. In our building alone, there were six other boys in his situation. They'd get together at the end of the day to chat out in the hall.

One evening, when I was playing with my sisters in front of the building, Malek Raihan, a neighbor, rushed over and told me to warn Daoud that an army patrol was in the area. I ran to alert my brother and his friends, who all hurried home to the hiding places their parents had fixed up inside their apartments. My mother really tore into Daoud that day. Under no circumstances was he to leave the apartment! He didn't even attend two wedding receptions given by close relatives of ours. At that time, even pop and folk music dealt with the issues of military service and the army, and women would sing these songs at weddings.

The wind blows and carries off my scarf,
The patrol has taken my beloved away,
May God put an end to these patrols,
That have taken my faithful beloved away!

There were all sorts of crazy rumors about these patrols. A neighbor told us that in the Parwan neighborhood, where soldiers were searching homes to find young men, one family told them that their son had just died, which was a ruse, because the boy was stretched out on his bed only pretending to be dead. Then the parents supposedly discovered that he really had died.

There were hundreds of stories like that in Kabul. Each family had its own tale to tell. And families could be torn between loyalty to the resistance and support of the government, with some members on either side. Should an Afghan in the Afghan army fight under the Soviets against other Afghans? Should an Afghan be pro-Soviet or anti-Soviet? Or neutral? It was hard to be neutral when sons reached draft age—an age the government kept changing at will, depending on the army's needs.

At one birthday party, the guests began singing quatrains in the traditional fashion. There were families from Kohestan, a plain about thirty miles north of the capital, and other families who lived in Kabul. And the verses went back and forth within the same extended family, between those who approved of the Communist regime and those from Kohestan who supported the resistance. The pro-Communists sang:

Oh what a fine and proud young man
Standing on a tank as he heads for the front,
On a tank that is going to the Panshir Valley!
While our women's eyes are bright with tears . . .

And the resistance sympathizers countered with:

I was surrounded by flowers and a mujahid called to me
I am grateful for his kindness—he offered me some tea,
Let him keep his tea, and I give him my thanks,
I adore this brave warrior with his gun on his shoulder!

At the end of the winter, the press announced that high school graduates could register at the university and take the competitive entrance examinations. Military patrols would be out in the city that day as usual, however, rounding up and questioning students. There were more checkpoints than ever, and more soldiers manning them.

Wahid took Daoud and a few other students from the neighborhood over in his own jeep, because army jeeps weren't stopped by the patrols. That wasn't enough to escape the dragnet, though, because the boys' examination papers were graded harder than the girls' exams: The government was doing its best to ensure that it would get its hands on the largest possible number of young men.

We waited anxiously all day. Daoud finally came home at the end of the afternoon, looking pleased. He had reason to be hopeful, because he was second in his class at the high school. He had chosen economics as his specialty and had passed the entrance exam. At that time, when a male student was enrolled at the university, he received a student card and an army certificate of exemption from military service. This certificate was valid for three months and was renewed at the end of each trimester if the student passed his examinations, but it was canceled if he failed.

At the end of the first trimester, Daoud was at the head of his class. Ordinarily, like all good students, he would have been given a scholarship to continue his studies in the U.S.S.R. He had no desire whatsoever to go there, but Papa wanted him to leave Kabul to avoid having to join the army. Since Daoud wasn't a party member, however, he was given no scholarship at all. He argued with the secretary of the Communist Youth Organization responsible for awarding the scholarships and was told simply, "There's nothing for you!"

Finally my father went to see the secretary to press his son's case, complaining so loudly about this injustice that Daoud was awarded a scholarship in the end, but one valid only in the Republic of Tajikistan, in Dushanbe instead of Moscow. Daoud accepted it anyway, and left to study economics in Dushanbe.

And it was lucky for him that he did, because the rules for compulsory military service changed overnight: Without warning, all male students—whether ordinary citizens or the sons of government ministers—found themselves required to serve a six-month stint in the army. The authorities had decided that depending on the army's needs at the time, every man had to serve a total of two years in the military. Fortunately, Daoud was in Tajikistan.

We wrote to him; now and then he would call us at home. After a year he came back to spend his holidays in Kabul and described to us the misery and hardship he'd seen in Dushanbe. Our leaders here were telling us wonderful things about the Soviet people, who were actually living in grim poverty.

"I met a woman who worked on a state farm for two rubles a day. The professors over there will give you a good grade in exchange for a key chain, and you can pay your student expenses for a year by selling a pair of jeans in Dushanbe. All the Afghan students arrive with jeans, sunglasses, umbrellas—anything at all, because anything you can find here or in Peshawar is worth a fortune there. Even a nail clipper, or a package of chewing gum!"

In the student community of Tajikistan, Daoud said that all things Soviet were in fashion.

"The richest guys marry Russian women and give Russian names to their children, like Natasha, Treshkova, Valentina, Alexis, Ivan. That's part of the program to sovietize society. They send young Tajiks to Moscow and replace them with real Russians."

He also explained to us that this sovietization of Tajikistan had brought the Tajiks a huge problem of national identity, even though they had won their independence from Moscow in 1991.

When he next came home on holiday, in August 1992, Daoud returned to a Kabul no longer under Communist control: The regime had fallen in April, driven out by the alliance of mujahideen. The fundamentalist Hekmatyar was still hammering away at us, however, showering rockets on Kabul.

This month of vacation was difficult for Daoud, because he'd forgotten how to deal with rocket fire. He couldn't understand why we weren't terrified like he was. Sadly, we were used to it.

We stayed in the room on the east side of the apartment to avoid the line of fire. One day, at around one o'clock, we'd just finished lunch and were having tea while watching television when two rockets landed right across from our building. We always left our windows open to keep them from being shattered, so they were spared, but our neighbors' windows broke into smithereens.

We ran to hide in the hall, the only place in the apartment that was safe from flying glass. This time I was crying, and Daoud as well. The explosions had started a fire quite close by, and the apartment was beginning to burn. We threw buckets of water everywhere to put out the flames and had only just finished when Wahid returned. He had gone down to the street at the first sounds of rocket fire.

"Is everyone all right?"

Mama and Daoud were frantic.

"Where were you?" they screamed. "What were you doing outside at a time like that?"

"It's war. I went out to help the neighbors—all the men came down to put out the fire. Some people were wounded, and one was killed."

A neighbor, a man who had recently gotten married, had been hit in the back by flying glass.

In the room we'd been in at the beginning of the explosions, the mosquito netting at the window was slashed into a dozen holes.

The mujahideen units stationed in the neighborhood

had helped everyone extinguish the blaze and take the victims to the hospital. Two hours later, the electricity was cut. We listened to the news on our transistor radio: More than a hundred and fifty rockets had fallen that day, injuring the same number of people and leaving twenty dead. Daoud had his ear glued to the radio.

"I want to get out of Kabul," he told us. "I want to go back to school."

In spite of the fighting, the very next day he went to the Ministry of Foreign Affairs, asked for his visa, bought a plane ticket, and a week later flew off for Dushanbe, via Tashkent. When he'd left to come home on vacation, they'd told him that the new Afghan government hated the Soviet Union, that the authorities in Kabul wouldn't let him return to Tajikistan. He wasn't the only student in this position. But the Ministry of Foreign Affairs had no objection to his departure, as long as his studies were paid for in advance by the Soviets.

Daoud stayed in Dushanbe until September 1992. When he came home for good he was twenty-three years old, Commander Massoud's forces were still in control of Kabul, and Hekmatyar's fundamentalists, determined to reclaim the city from him, were hurling rockets at us in an appalling civil war.

Boys could no longer climb up on the roofs to search the skies eagerly for kites. They still can't, since the Taliban have forbidden the little boys of Kabul to fly kites. Some day they'll even wind up forbidding birds to fly.

We've been at war now for twenty years. Almost four years of house arrest! In the year 2000 I'll be twenty. Will the war still be raging? Daoud's friends say in their letters that the world is forgetting us, that we live at the bottom of a hole, that the Taliban have achieved their objective and are welcoming more Pakistani volunteers to their military training camps every day.

The BBC says the Americans bombed these camps in retaliation for an attack against their embassies in Africa.

But the permanent attack being mounted against us, the men and women of Afghanistan, doesn't interest them at all.

The BBC also says that opium is an important source of revenue for the Taliban government, which levies a 20 percent tax on the shipments of drug traffickers.

Our country is in the hands of organized bandits. In the beginning Papa urged us to never lose hope. "In two weeks," he would say. "In three months, in six months." And now—in how many years?

I think about the thousands of future *talibs* growing up all around us.

Poor little boys, and poor Afghanistan! Those kites once looked so lovely in our skies.

SEVEN

Who Speaks for Afghanistan?

Whenever we turn the dial on our transistor and get Radio Sharia, we hear truly chilling things. Such as this logic: Since it is unjust to deprive someone of liberty, the amputation of a hand is a much more charitable punishment for a thief than prison. That way the thief can return to his job and support his family. But if a child steals bread tomorrow in the streets of Kabul because his widowed mother has no male protector, is forbidden to work, and is thus condemned to beg, whose hand will the Taliban cut off?

There are thieves, and then there are thieves. According to a Taliban decree, a man who dares "change afghani bills of small denominations into larger ones" is also a "thief." And just what is this so-called thief guilty of doing? Lightening his pockets of the weight of inflation? Hiding his savings from other thieves?

Word on the street has it that Mullah Omar never goes anywhere without trunks full of afghanis, Pakistani rupees, and American dollars. No one knows if this is his personal fortune or the state treasury. The Taliban state is not our Afghanistan. Their Islamic emirate doesn't have anything to do with our Islam.

The BBC and the Voice of America aren't talking much about our country, at the moment. Daoud is right: We're living like rats in a hole inaccessible to the rest of the world. In August 1999, however, the radio mentions an offensive by General Massoud's forces that pushes back the Taliban on the Shamali Plain, north of Kabul.

"As long as it hasn't dawned on the world that the Taliban are actually the creation of Pakistan, we'll never get out of this," says Daoud glumly. "Everybody supports Pakistan, and Pakistan wants the Taliban to keep a stranglehold on us, so what can an isolated mujahid like Massoud do? Permanent civil war is no solution. In any case, there is no solution, except for exile."

I think of my brother Wahid, living in Moscow. He has told us he got married to a young Russian named Natasha on April 1, 2000, another wedding we couldn't attend.

What side would he have chosen if my parents hadn't urged him to leave the country? When the Taliban arrived in the capital, some Kabulis believed they were saviors who would restore peace to our land, end the factional infighting that was destroying Kabul, and reestablish the rules of Islam. Would my brother have thought so too?

True, rockets aren't raining down on us anymore, but the city is drowning in a deathly silence. And the pro-Taliban supporters here must have quickly realized they'd been fooled. The peace they had in mind was not the loss of their traditional customs: no more tambourines, or singing, or dancing at weddings, or kites, or sports with pigeons—or else the pigeons will have their throats cut! Still another decree . . .

The "street radio" tells us (but is this true?) that Mullah Omar is afraid of Kabul and lives in a house in Kandahar built for him by his father-in-law bin Laden. As for Radio Sharia, it announces that this bin Laden has offered to build and supply bakeries in Kabul, a function formerly carried out by the UN.

When the UN Security Council imposed sanctions on the Taliban at the end of 1999 because they refused to extradite bin Laden to the United States, which had accused him of terrorism, bin Laden warned, "The earthquakes and tempests of God will strike you, and you will be surprised by your fate."

In 1996, when I passed part of my journalism exam, the unknown Saudi was financing the construction of mosques. Mosques and bread are two pillars of daily life in Kabul. That's how he's becoming important in the country. I wonder what else he will finance. I'd like to illustrate an article on this bin Laden in an issue of our review *Dawn*, but that's impossible: There are no portraits of him in Kabul, no pictures, because they are forbidden.

Collecting interesting items for our review poses certain problems. Farida reports on rumors going around the marketplace, Daoud hears whispered gossip in the stores, but there's not much to write about here on the eve of the millennium, when the rest of the world will be throwing a huge party.

Before, we used to celebrate the New Year, too, but the Taliban have decided that this is a pagan ritual! Even the Spring Festival has been banished. Are flowers pagan? Soraya, with her collection of flower postcards—is she an outlaw?

The year 2000 brings us nothing new for our magazine except . . . *Titanic*. For the millennium issue of *Dawn* we find a treasure trove of thoroughly heathen material. Daoud brings us a poster of Leonardo DiCaprio and even unearths a video of the film from Pakistan. Small shops set up in the dry bed of the Kabul River, which is often transformed by drought into a bazaar, are selling *Titanic* tie-ins. The black market is going crazy over that movie. *Titanic* style is all the rage, especially with barbers: Radio Sharia announces that twenty-eight of them have been arrested and convicted for giving young men Leonardo DiCaprio haircuts.

TVs and VCRs are on in the basements of Kabulis, who rebel as best they can. The city is unarmed, its women walk with bent heads, its men bow beneath the lash, and yet they secretly lap up the steamy love story of *Titanic* and weep over the hero's death beneath the ocean waves. This might seem silly and shallow, because daily life is horrible, the country is starving, refugees from the countryside are crowding into camps on the borders of Pakistan and Iran, and women beggars are flooding the streets of Kandahar, Kabul, Herat, Mazar-i-Sharif, and Jalalabad. But the Taliban don't talk about these dire issues—they're too busy imprisoning barbers, whipping men, and beating up women. So, since men as well as women are forbidden by law to laugh in the streets, and children are forbidden to play, everyone sheds tears over a heathen love story.

Leonardo is so cute! The girls in my neighborhood need to "sin" by gazing at him. I glue his photo into *Dawn* with the feeling of rebellion one has at twenty years old, robbed of education and learning, robbed of life.

The special *Titanic* issue is finished at last. Daoud has done the title in his beautiful handwriting. I'm unaware as yet that this will be our last homemade edition. January 1, 2001, begins sadly under the oppressive rule of the Taliban. We're cheered to receive at last, via a long string of messengers, a color photograph of Wahid's marriage: My brother is wearing a suit and tie, with a white flower in his buttonhole; his wife, prettily made up, is in a dress of white lace with an off-the-shoulder neckline, wearing a delicate white veil over blond hair done in a chignon. They are a handsome couple. On the back of the photo Wahid has written: "Dear Mama, this is for you. Our wedding picture."

Wahid looks so happy. Where he is, no *talib* came to smash the photographer's camera. His young bride doesn't risk being whipped for showing off her beauty. They are free, and we are in prison.

The Taliban control almost all the country. Winter is here; Afghans are fleeing the cold and hunger. Daoud reports that the Pakistani police are demanding money from every Afghan trying to cross the border, even the wretches desperate to escape the famine.

Pakistan wants our death and is not far from getting it. We're completely isolated. The Taliban shut down the offices of the UN Special Mission in Kabul a long time ago. They've cut us off from the international scene in a nightmare that will never end. The BBC speaks of massacres of Afghan civilians in several villages occupied by the Taliban.

The Voice of America is worried about the Buddhas of Bamiyan, an archaeological marvel so famous in Afghanistan that it appears on the airplane tickets of Aryana Airlines. Daoud sees them every day, at the ticket counter where he works. These Buddhas have been the pride of the Hazarajat region for centuries. After destroying the artworks of the Museum of Kabul and the frescoes of Behzad, a famous Persian painter of the fifteenth century, in Herat, the lovely city founded by Alexander the Great in the fourth century B.C. and the capital of the Mongol Tamerlane—now the Taliban are attacking the Buddhas! Even the English and the Russians had respected the rich cultural heritage of Afghanistan. Tourists used to flock to Bamiyan and Herat.

Radio Sharia announces that in accordance with the decree of Mullah Omar ordering the destruction of all statuary antedating the birth of Islam, the Buddhas of Bamiyan will be destroyed.

The Voice of America broadcasts an interview with an authority from the international archaeological community, who rails against the massacre of these colossi dating from the fifth century A.D. that belong to the entire world, as well as an interview with a spokesperson for Mullah Omar justifying their destruction because they represent heathen gods.

"The Islamic Emirate of Afghanistan cannot tolerate idols, and these statues represent no faith recognized by Islam. We are only breaking up some stones."

In another broadcast of the Voice of America, the Taliban's spokesperson says that he cannot confirm whether the Buddhas have been demolished or not. He hints that the rebels of the Northern Alliance might have gotten there first . . . and then he claims credit for this crime against culture.

At Bamiyan, the people know. They saw the Taliban shoot their machine guns and rocket-launchers at the two colossi that had stood ensconced in their massive shrines for fifteen centuries. According to the BBC, the whole world is in shock at this act of vandalism that would be rivaled only by the destruction of an Egyptian pyramid.

The Taliban have not reprinted the plane tickets of Aryana Airlines; the image of the colossi remains.

The worst news on the BBC now, in February 2001, is the announcement of a visit to Paris by the Minister of Health, Mullah Mohammed Abbas, who will discuss humanitarian issues in France. Radio Sharia is delighted at the idea of this official trip! The announcer claims that it means the recognition of the Taliban state.

A *talib* in Paris, in the country of the rights of man . . . A "Minister of Health" who bars women from hospitals, who in 1997 dared imprison the European Commissioner for Humanitarian Affairs! Emma Bonino, who had come to visit an NGO (nongovernmental agency) in need of emergency financial aid in Kabul, was roughed up, beaten in front of the foreign cameraman accompanying her, and questioned for hours before being released. What right has this *talib* to go abroad to discuss humanitarian matters? Everyone knows that the refugee camps are neglected, that the drought, the winter weather, and the relentless attacks of the Taliban, particularly in the north, are grinding those poor people into the dust.

Farida, Soraya, and I are furious and disgusted. The French should have invited one of our women doctors or nurses, now forbidden to work under the Taliban, whereas they once formed the very core of our hospitals, the Ministry of Health, and the daycare centers, and were indispensable to the effort to introduce modern practices of maternal and infant hygiene to the countryside and provide emergency gynecological care. This visit is a *disgrace*. This *talib* is only an uneducated mullah; he's not even a doctor, he's just a Pakistani puppet. It's a staggering blow for Mama, who's been heartsick over this situation for such a long time. This *talib* has been received not only by the Ministry of Foreign Affairs but also by the President of the National Assembly. It's so awful that we're in a frenzy of outrage at home. And we also feel as though we are sinking still deeper into despair: If France is welcoming a *talib*, that means the Taliban propaganda has worked.

"The French haven't met with anyone from the resistance, they never even sent a journalist to denounce what's going on in Kabul—and they receive a *talib*! We're really done for."

Meanwhile, two Afghan women found guilty of adultery are executed in the sports stadium of Kabul. Ten unfaithful husbands are flogged. And there's an earthquake in Faisalabad, in the south of Pakistan. The tremors reach all the way up to Kabul, causing some panic.

I think that we Afghans know more about earthquakes than the Taliban do about the Koran.

April 2001. This time the Voice of America and the BBC announce the arrival in Paris of General Ahmed Shah Massoud, commander of the resistance in the Panshir Valley.

According to Farida, who's always up on the latest news, the "street radio" says that Kabulis are in an unbelievable ferment of excitement. People have even been seen in public listening to their transistors turned up as loud as possible, which is absolutely forbidden. And when a *talib* swoops down with his threatening whip, the delinquent replies: "But it's not music! It's not an Iranian station! I'm simply listening to Radio Sharia."

Sometimes a kind of madness can overwhelm fear. At last, Paris is welcoming an Afghan, but will Paris listen to him?

At first Radio Sharia denies everything: "Massoud did not leave for Paris. It's a trick!" Then, realizing that all the forbidden radios—and they know that we listen to them in secret every evening—are talking about nothing else, they try to spin the event to their advantage. "This rebel is just over there begging for arms to bring back with him. But we'll beat him in spite of France's weapons!"

The rebel is received by the Minister of Foreign Affairs, then invited to the European Parliament as a kind of ambassador. This is the first time something is finally happening outside the Taliban walls. It's too much to say that we're bursting with hope, but like all Kabulis, we stay tuned to the BBC, which unfortunately isn't giving many details. Massoud has spoken at length with the French minister Hubert Védrine, and he has read a declaration to the European Parliament in Strasbourg asking that Europe send representatives to evaluate the humanitarian situation in Afghanistan and see for themselves the human rights violations being committed by the Taliban.

Almost at the same time, Dr. Sima, who has set up her underground clinic in Kabul, sends a message to Mama.

"The French are looking for women who would fly to Paris to talk about our plight in Afghanistan. A French organization and a women's magazine want to launch an information campaign. I can't go there myself, though—I'm needed too much here. So I told the French organization to contact you. It would be good if Latifa could go there to talk about what she's seen, the way women are persecuted, the secret schools. Such testimony is the only way we can resist. And you should go with her; you're my friend, you've been a doctor, and you can't practice anymore because of the Taliban. The two of you should go there—it's important! The first people you'll meet will be journalists. It's a magazine called *Elle* and it's quite well known. And you'll be able to ask questions at the European Parliament, you'll see influential people, like Mme. Nicole Fontaine. You can't pass up this chance!"

I'd like to go, but I'm afraid. First of all, I've never traveled in the West, never taken a plane. I've been living shut up at home since I was sixteen. Why did Dr. Sima pick me? Farida, Maryam, and I are not the only ones running underground schools.

Even though she's still unwell and quite weak, Mama is leaning toward going.

"Dr. Sima is right. It's important for the West to know that women doctors are condemned to stay home and can't help the sick at all anymore."

Soraya approves, too, although she's worried about the risks of traveling that far from home.

"Listen, Latifa: Life is so hard here—this might mean something could change for us! You'll meet important people; Dr. Sima said so."

My father agrees completely about how vital it is to tell people what's happening here, but he's torn between the necessity of accompanying us, since we'll need a *mah-*

ram with a passport to travel, and his anxiety over leaving Daoud at home with Marie and Soraya.

"The only problem is our family's safety. If the Taliban learn about this while some of us are in Paris and the rest are in Kabul, we might very well be separated permanently and have to face a dangerous situation."

We make our decision after talking things over with some friends. So: Mama, Papa, and I will leave, along with another young woman, Diba, who also runs a clandestine school. One of her male cousins will go with her to Islamabad using his own passport. We quickly organize everything. We'll take a minibus to Peshawar, and the visas from our last trip to Pakistan are still valid.

On April 28, at five in the morning, the taxi is waiting for us downstairs to take us to the bus station. Diba and her cousin will join us in Pakistan, because they still have a visa and passport problem to resolve.

Officially, we're going to Pakistan—like the last time—to take Mama to the hospital. Leaving behind Soraya, Daoud, and Marie, their eyes brimming with tears, is so very hard. And the trip will be difficult, with that constant fear of being turned back or arrested for no reason, and now this secret we must all keep. There's nothing to give away our final destination, of course. Our instructions are simple: We're to go to Peshawar, then to Islamabad, and once we've reached the Pakistani capital, we're to telephone the Afghan embassy in Paris to find out where to pick up our prepaid plane tickets. Then we'll go to the French embassy in Islamabad to obtain French visas. Finally, if all goes well, we'll fly on Emirates Airlines to Dubai, and on to Paris.

My stomach is in knots at the border, where we wait forty-five minutes before crossing. The Pakistanis make the passengers—Hazaras—on another minibus get out while they check everyone's passports, taking their sweet time, but at last the travelers are allowed through.

Once across the border, we travel on to Peshawar, where we check into a hotel for one day. I've no idea how Diba's cousin managed to obtain a passport and Pakistani visa for the two of them so quickly, but they join us in good time.

I have the phone number of the Afghan embassy in Paris written on a piece of paper. When I call, the person who answers takes precautions: She doesn't speak clearly, uses innocuous phrases, asks me who I am, if everyone is there, says we'll call you back tomorrow. I have the impression they are verifying our identity, as if they're afraid the phone is tapped. I hang up, and we wait until the next day.

This time, the message is clear: "You can leave now! Write down the name and address of the travel agency and the ticket numbers. The tickets will be waiting for you there."

Off to Islamabad, a three-hour trip. I've never been

to the capital of Pakistan, but I haven't the heart to look around like a tourist; this is such a big adventure for me that I'm braced for anything, even the worst.

First worry: The man at the agency frowns in irritation at the ticket numbers I give him.

"These numbers don't match the tickets you want. There are no reservations with these numbers."

We leave, feeling increasingly anxious. What if it's a trap, a way of testing our identities? I've no idea—we have to telephone Paris again and see if there's an explanation.

"Ah . . . I'm so sorry, it's a mistake. You weren't given the correct ticket numbers. Write these down."

Back to the agency. This time, we get the tickets.

Now we can go to the French embassy for our visas. When we get there, I'm surprised by the crowd of people waiting. Someone is expecting us, but who? How do we jump the line?

When I ask a guard, in Urdu, he tells me: "Make an appointment!"

Then I speak to another one near the doors, telling him in careful English that I'm supposed to see someone inside. He understands immediately.

"Yes, you have an appointment, someone's waiting for you. You may go in."

The man escorts us inside, speaks to someone, and telephones to announce our arrival.

A few minutes later, we find ourselves in the office of a French official who counts us with a faint expression of surprise, then speaks in English to Diba's cousin. My English isn't nearly as good as his, but I can follow their conversation.

"There are five of you, and only four are leaving. Why is there someone extra? I wasn't informed of this!"

"I'm not leaving with the others. I only brought my cousin here."

Reassured, the official hands us forms to fill out for the visas.

"You don't have to write in everything, just put down the important information. How long will you need to stay in France?"

"A week, or ten days, that would be better."

In a few minutes our French visas are all in order, while it will take months for the people waiting outside to get one, if they ever do. And it's most unusual to obtain visas for four people all at the same time.

The man wishes us a pleasant journey and shows us out.

We're over the first hurdle. The second one is at the airport in Islamabad, where Diba's cousin says goodbye to us. We go through various formalities and present our passports to have the visas checked.

The policeman gives us a funny look. I'm terrified.

"That's unusual . . . Two passports and four visas?

How did that happen? How did you get these visas? It's strange that the French embassy would issue four visas like that. Very strange . . ."

We've got our answer ready: "We're going to see some young Afghan women in France. This gentleman is my father; he's going with us."

"What young women? Why? Tell me the truth, what's this all about? What are you going to do with these people?"

"We're going to visit an association for young Afghan women. My father's going with us."

He frowns and goes off looking for someone. I am so afraid that he'll go through my bag and find our *chadris*, which would prove that we're traveling from Afghanistan; we had to wear them before we crossed into Pakistan, and of course we'll need them when we return. We wouldn't be the first young women to be stopped because of this. Well, if he finds them, so what; I'll just tell him we're used to wearing them and he can keep them if he wants.

I look around for someone to help us, anyone. There's a man wearing an airport personnel uniform, so I timidly try him.

"Excuse me, sir, this is my first airplane trip, and I'm a little nervous. Would you please tell that policeman not to be so strict with us?"

"I'll talk to him—that guy can be really annoying."

He walks over to the policeman, who is speaking

with a second policeman not far away. Meanwhile, another passenger tells my father that the first officer is angling for some money.

"I won't pay; I haven't enough money. I can't spare any. If he won't let us through, then we don't go."

The airport employee returns with the first policeman.

"Look at her," he says with a smile. "What harm could she possibly do? She's young; she's my daughter's age. Leave her alone."

The policeman gives back our passports and visas. We can go through the checkpoint, but Papa notices that the customs policeman is still keeping a sullen eye on us. He checks the other passengers' passports without paying too much attention. I turn my back to him so as not to become even more anxious.

"Don't worry," Papa reassures us. "Our papers are perfectly in order. Everything's fine, he can't do a thing."

It's a long wait: an hour in that room with that man constantly staring at us. It's as if he were trying to think of some way to catch us after all.

To our relief, we finally move into the departure lounge. There are restrooms and a restaurant where we can have some tea.

I'm concerned about Mama; I hope she will bear up under this tiring trip and the stress of our "secret mission." The flight to Paris is announced. The bus is waiting for us on the tarmac. We still have to get to the plane, cross this last stretch of Pakistani soil and all the anguish it represents—and as long as the plane is still on the ground, I will be afraid. Even when we're sitting in our seats, when I should be more relaxed, I feel dizzy, and as the motors roar and the plane lifts off, my head is spinning. I feel so weak and helpless.

We're seated in the middle of the plane, which is fine with me—I don't want to see Pakistan even from the air. Our first stop is Dubai, where we'll change planes before going on to Paris. I have to focus my mind on that: going on to Paris.

The stopover in Dubai is horrible. The other passengers all get on the next plane, but we're still having our papers thoroughly studied by a policeman.

"You! Stand aside. Wait here!"

So we wait, and it starts all over again. I ought to call the French embassy here. No, that's not being reasonable. In the end, I do call, only to warn them that we've no idea if we'll be able to fly out of Dubai.

Mama reminds me what to say this time if I'm questioned: "Tell them I'm ill, that we're going to France to get medical attention for me."

The policeman stares at me stonily.

"Where are your medical documents?"

"In our luggage, on the plane."

"What doctor are you going to see?"

"We don't know yet."

"How can that be? You don't know anyone there? It's your first trip; there aren't any other stamps on this passport. Your father has no job listed on this passport. How did you pay for this trip?"

"We sold the house to pay for the tickets and my mother's medical care."

"You sold the house? So you're not coming back?"

"Of course we are. If we weren't coming back, we would have brought along all our things, instead of packing only enough for a week."

"You have money for the medical expenses?"

"My father has four hundred dollars, and a few Pakistani rupees."

"What if that's not enough?"

"My father will have more sent from Pakistan."

He counts our money, checks our tickets.

"Stay here. I don't get this; these aren't ordinary visas."

Aside from one Japanese man, we are the only ones left. Another policeman shows up, I repeat my explanations, and he goes off to phone I don't know whom. Then he returns.

"All right. You can go."

When the plane takes off for Paris, I slump in my seat like a rag doll. Better not think about what the return trip will be like.

In Paris, everything is simple. The chargé d'affaires at the embassy is waiting for us, and he introduces us to the Frenchwomen who have organized this entire trip: Marie-Françoise and Catherine from *Elle* magazine, along with Shékéba, president of the Free Afghanistan Association, who will be our guide and translator, and Myriam, who accompanies her.

Mama, who knows three words of French, says "Bonjour." I don't even know how to say that! Shékéba explains to us that there were no cameras or photographers at the airport for security reasons, and that we will have to use false names here in France. From now on my name is Latifa, and that's the name I will use to tell my story.

When we leave the airport, our first image of Paris is those tall buildings I've never seen before except in films. Next, the Eiffel Tower. I expected to find Paris magnificent, and that's just what it is: magnificent.

We plunge into a whirlwind—first a hotel, then a television studio, where they promise me my face will be blurry on the screen so that no one can identify me. I speak shyly at first during the interview, while Shékéba translates my words.

The next day, we take the train to Brussels and the European Parliament: So here we are, Mama, Diba, and I, ambassadors for the women of our poor country.

Shékéba tells me about General Massoud's visit to

Paris, which she obviously knows a lot more about than I do. He asked for humanitarian assistance from the Minister of Foreign Affairs but received only symbolic support, no promise of direct aid. In Strasbourg, where he met with Nicole Fontaine, the president of the European Parliament, he asked not for arms or foreign troops in Afghanistan, but for the French to support the resistance movement against the Taliban and put pressure on the regime to negotiate a peace agreement and find a political settlement. Mme. Fontaine found General Massoud to be an effective voice on behalf of any future peace process in Afghanistan.

Massoud then went to Brussels to meet with the European Union High Representative for Common Foreign and Security Policy, Javier Solana.

Shékéba makes it clear to me that General Massoud did not receive much in the way of support in Brussels. However, the newspaper *Courrier International* published an appeal signed by him, in which he summarized the history of the border dispute between Afghanistan and Pakistan and spoke of the latter's desire to increase its regional power by "satellitizing" Afghanistan, thus gaining direct access to Central Asia.

"The Taliban have massacred thousands of people because of their ethnic and religious affiliations in what can only be called a program of ethnic cleansing. Afghanistan is facing a terrible tragedy that may well affect the entire region, given that the Pakistanis and the Taliban support and compose a terrorist network that threatens their neighbors. I would have hoped that after our victory over Communism, we would have earned the gratitude of other nations and some help in binding up our wounds. Unfortunately, Pakistan stabbed us in the back, Washington put its trust in Islamabad, and Europe chose to be indifferent to our plight. To bring an end to this tragedy, the international community can increase its humanitarian aid to the Afghan people, on the one hand, and on the other, use their influence to put a halt to Pakistan's meddling in Afghanistan."

While men talk about politics, Mama, Diba, and I speak only about women, and how we have been robbed of our voices and our rights, oppressed as the designated victims of a systematic purge. We are no longer able to work, to learn, to show ourselves, left widows and beggars in a country where many men have been killed, handicapped, or exiled by twenty years of war, and have no more weapons with which to fight the Taliban.

One day, who knows, the purge will reach its climax, and we'll see women subjected to the ultimate degradation of a noble and ancient land: forced to bring into this world the sons of the Taliban. I must—all three of us must—fight back, must say that we refuse to give up our dignity, that we want to bring back from France the freedom that I have never known in my twenty years on this earth. We are a proud people, in a land rich with history, and it is there, to them, that I would like to take this freedom.

So Shékéba and our little troop in *chadris* have made the rounds of important people. Nicole Fontaine, Raymond Forni in the National Assembly, Christian Poncelet in the Senate, and Charles Josselin, the Minister of Cooperation.

I arrived with my parents and Diba on May 2, 2001. We were to have left for home ten days later, but the "ambassadors' tour" lasted longer than expected, so we had to extend our visas.

By the end of May, I feel disappointed. If I hadn't met the journalists from *Elle*, if I hadn't seen them cry, support us, love us, and demonstrate in the streets, I would almost be sorry that I came on this mission to speak for the women of Afghanistan. Because I don't think anything will change. My father, ever the optimist, keeps telling me that we're lucky to have seen France, to have met all these people, and that a word is never lost in the desert. One day it will burst into bloom.

"You haven't done all this for nothing. Just wait. Women listen to other women, and what you've told them will make people here understand what the Taliban are doing to you. A woman is not nothing. If a *talib* tells a woman that she is nothing and he is everything, he is ignorant. Man is born of woman, the saint has a mother, the whole world was born in the body of a woman. You should remember this Afghan saying: 'If the pearl tells the oyster it is nothing, and the pearl is everything, then a fish can tell the sky to stop raining.' "

On the last day of May, we receive a fax at the embassy, sent by Daoud from Pakistan. He warns us that the Taliban have issued a fatwa against all women who denounce their regime. He has also learned that some *talibs* have gutted our apartment. He doesn't dare go see for himself, and besides some neighbors have gotten word to him that *talibs* have already moved into our home.

We've lost everything. All our mementos, our family photos, my uncle's paintings that Mama hid so carefully—everything our family had in Mikrorayan is gone.

The look on the faces of my mother and father, as they stare into the void of our past, is like a knife in my heart. I feel that it's my fault. Now we cannot go back home to Kabul.

An embassy employee confirms the disaster.

"They've launched a fatwa against you without even knowing who you are. They say that these women in France are just lying and that if they come back, the Taliban will kill them. The text of the fatwa is on the Internet."

After all our efforts have come to this! Now even my father is demoralized.

"Yes, they welcomed you to France. You met people, it's true, but where did it get you?"

I'm devastated. From now on, there will be the uncertainty of renewing our visas, the search for places to stay with other refugees, and those questions going round and round in our heads, questions without answers. I'm here, alive? But what will happen to me? I find myself in a country where I don't speak the language. Mama is adrift in her world of calamity and mute suffering. My father has lost all he had, two of his children are in Pakistan, another in Russia, another in the United States. The family is broken up, scattered. Only I am with him, the last of his daughters. How can I continue my education? Where will we live from now on? Where will we start over? And *what* will we start over?

The future will prove to us, however, that we aren't alone. We'll have the support of the Afghan community, of our embassy, and of course, of our friends at *Elle*, who will help us cope with red tape and finding a place to stay.

I am given the opportunity to write this book. I still have this hope: To explain how a girl from Kabul, educated first during the Soviet occupation, then under Communist regimes throughout four years of civil war, was finally locked away by a monstrous power, her life confiscated when she was only sixteen.

Other Afghans have never stopped fighting, are still fighting, in my country. I know that the refugees on the borders of Afghanistan's neighbors endure hardships much worse than mine. What can I do—except tell you what my life has been like in the city of Kabul, a city of rubble and ruins?

September 9, 2001: At his headquarters in the Panshir Valley, General Massoud is the victim of two suicide bombers posing as Arab journalists. No one knows if he is dead or alive.

September 11: America is attacked.

September 13: The death of Ahmed Shah Massoud is revealed.

October 7: The Americans go to war against the Taliban.

I've come to the end of my story, at a time when weapons are speaking in our place. As always. *Azadi* means freedom in our language. But who speaks for Afghanistan?

I don't know anymore.

Afterword: A Dream of Peace and Democracy

December 2001

As the black turbans of the Taliban fade away, as we slowly awaken from our nightmares, we should speak of hope and of the freedom we may once more enjoy. And I do speak of these things.

I should return to Afghanistan to embrace my country wholeheartedly, now that I have seen on television that women are showing their faces again and men are flocking to barbers to have their beards shaved off. I've heard the sound of laughter in Kabul. I won't go home until kites replace the bombers in the sky over Kandahar, but I will be going home.

We should be delighted that the representatives of each ethnic group at the Bonn Conference—Tajiks, Uzbeks, Pashtuns, Hazaras—have promised to give steadfast support to a provisional government and accept UN aid for the rebuilding of a land that has experienced a devastation almost unparalleled in the history of the world. And I am delighted by the success of the conference.

Wahid, my eldest brother, is eager to leave Moscow and come home. We don't know whether my brother Daoud, his wife, and my sister Soraya are in Pakistan or Afghanistan; we haven't heard from them in a long time, and I'm worried. As for me, I am an exile at the moment, but a privileged one who has enough to eat, shelter from the chill of winter, and who has finally been able to speak to the West about the plight of her country. So I can freely express my instinctive fear about the future—and that is another privilege as well.

For centuries the men of my nation have received as boys not childish toys, but knives, muskets, rifles, and now, Kalashnikovs. For centuries, generation after generation, the master players on the great Afghan chessboard have kept changing, as though tribal wars were a national sport. And for centuries as well, our women have been born to wear the *chadri*. For centuries, international ambitions have maintained these traditions.

And so, to speak despite everything of hope, of the dream of peace and democracy to which my generation clings so ardently, I pray God that women may have a greater voice in the coming debates. Three women alongside thirty men in Bonn are not enough. I pray God that whoever will lead our country may be, in his heart, as much Pashtun as Tajik, as much Uzbek as Hazara. That his wife may counsel and assist him; that he may choose advisers of great character and wisdom. That books may replace weapons, that education may teach us to respect one another, that our hospitals may be worthy of their mission, and that our culture may be reborn from the ruins of our pillaged museums. That the camps of famished refugees may disappear from our borders, and that the bread the hungry eat may be kneaded by their own hands.

I will do more than pray, because when the last *talib* has put away his black turban and I can be a free woman in a free Afghanistan, I will take up my life there once more and do my duty as a citizen, as a woman, and I hope, as a mother.

One day a European friend translated this line from one of her country's songs for me: "Woman is the future of mankind." May God grant that in Afghanistan, above all, men soon sing those words as well.

LATIFA

Acknowledgments

I express my deep gratitude:

To *Elle* magazine, which helped us immeasurably when we left Afghanistan in May 2001 to come to France; to Valérie Toranian; and especially to Marie-Françoise Colombani, who defends our cause with great conviction;

To Shékéba Hachemi, who collaborated on the writing of this book and who has dedicated her life to the cause of Afghan women. The association she founded in France in 1994, Afghanistan Libre [Free Afghanistan], collects funds intended to finance the construction of schools and hospitals in our country;

To Hakim Saeed, who was a great help to me in translating my thoughts into French.

I would also like to warmly thank M. and Mme. Mastan and all my friends for their encouragement.

Glossary*

chador: a scarf worn by Muslim women to cover the head and shoulders.

chadri: a dark veil of opaque material sewn to a close-fitting cap, with an embroidered mesh peephole at eye level. Of variable length, this veil may cover the face and arms, or the entire body, in which case it is called a **burka**, which is worn only in the most distant provinces.

fatwa: a religious ruling given on a question of law by a recognized authority in a Muslim community. This judgment, which has the value of a decree, may even encompass a sentence of death.

jihad: a holy war to defend Islam or Muslims, but in its literal sense, the word means the "striving" of each individual for religious and moral perfection. [The Koranic phrase "striving in the path of God" has been interpreted to mean armed struggle for the defense or expansion of Muslim power.]

mahram: the male mentor of a woman; he may be her father, brother, husband, or, if need be, her cousin.

mujahideen (*singular*: **mujahid**): "those who struggle," members of the Afghan Islamic resistance during the Soviet occupa-

*[Material within brackets has been added by the translator.]

tion (1979–1989). [Originally backed by the United States and financed by Saudi Arabia (which later embraced the Taliban) during the successful jihad against the Soviets, the victorious mujahideen then plunged the country into a civil war between rival tribal leaders that culminated in the rise of the Taliban.]

mullah: a Muslim cleric.

pakol: a traditional Afghan cap with a rolled brim.

Pashtun: the largest ethnic group in Afghanistan, a country torn by rivalries among the Pashtun, Tajik, Hazara, Uzbek, Turkmen. [Farsiwan, Baluch, Aimaq, and others. The Pashtun account for about a third of Afghanistan's estimated population of 26 million people and predominate in the south, on either side of the border between Afghanistan and Pakistan. The Pashtun have their own tribal laws and often consider themselves Pashtun first, and Pakistani or Afghan second. Historically, Afghanistan's rulers have been drawn from this ethnic group; almost all the Taliban leaders are Pashtun, as is the exiled king, Mohammed Zahir Shah.]

Sharia: a collection of commandments taken from the sacred texts of Islam, which govern the religious, political, social, and personal lives of Muslims. [The Koran, the sayings of Mohammed, and centuries of interpretation by Muslim scholars and judges form the basis of Islamic law, which covers many issues handled in the West by civil, commercial, and criminal law.]

Taliban (*singular*: **talib**): religious students educated in the Koranic schools of Pakistan who follow the tenets of Deobandism. This orthodox Islamic school of thought, which preaches the rejection of all outside influence and a strict, repressive reading of the Koran, was founded at the end of the nineteenth century in Deoband, in the north of India, and supported by the British, who were looking for a religious counterweight to the Hindu faith.

A Brief Chronology

1919: The Declaration of Independence of Afghanistan.

1921: The Treaty of Kabul marks the end of British interference in Afghan affairs.

1933–1973: The reign of Mohammed Zahir Shah. [Now 87, the former Afghan king, who has lived in Rome since he was overthrown in a palace coup, has been encouraged by the United States and Pakistan to convene a Loya Jirga, a grand national council that would attempt to set up an interim government in post-Taliban Afghanistan.]

1959: Women are no longer required to wear the veil.

1964: Women obtain the right to vote.

1965: The first parliamentary elections.

1973: The monarchy is overthrown by Mohammed Daoud, who establishes the first Republic of Afghanistan and serves as its president.

1978: A coup d'état installs the second republic, a Communist regime, led by President Noor Mohammed Taraki and Prime Minister Hafizullah Amin. Reforms imposed on Afghan society, which remains conservatively traditional, lead to popular uprisings and the rise of Islamist movements, which destabilize the government.

1979: Soviet military intervention. The mujahideen organize their resistance and begin a guerrilla war against the Afghan army—which fights under the aegis of the Soviet army—that will last ten years.

The successive presidencies of Babrak Karmal (1979–1986) and Dr. Mohammed Najibullah (1986–1992). [Made president by the Soviets, Mohammed Najibullah was an Afghan Communist who remained in power until he was ousted by the mujahideen.]

April 1988: The United States, the U.S.S.R., Pakistan, and the government in Kabul sign a UN-sponsored agreement in Geneva setting up a timetable for the withdrawal of Soviet forces from Afghanistan.

1989: The last of the Soviet troops are evacuated from Afghanistan.

The beginning of the civil war among mujahideen forces of different ethnic backgrounds; the principal antagonists will be the Pashtun Gulbuddin Hekmatyar and the Tajik Ahmed Shah Massoud. [A notoriously ruthless warlord, Hekmatyar first came to the attention of the West as a student at Kabul University in the 1960s, when he led a militant Islamic student group that threw acid in the faces of unveiled women students. Massoud will later become the leader of the Northern Alliance, a loose coalition of ethnic minority political parties—mostly Tajiks, Uzbeks, and Hazaras—that will oppose the Taliban.]

March 1992: General Massoud takes control of the northern provinces.

April 1992: General Massoud's mujahideen capture Kabul. Sibghatullah Mojaddedi serves as President of the Islamic State of Afghanistan until June, when he is succeeded by Burhanuddin Rabbani. [Rabbani was the nominal head of the Afghan government-in-exile recognized by the United Nations, and he is the ranking political leader of the Northern Alliance.]

Civil war flares up again, this time between the forces of General Massoud and Islamic extremists supported by Pakistan. The Taliban achieve their first successes in the south with the capture of Kandahar in 1994. [Kandahar will later become the main stronghold of the Taliban and Osama bin Laden's Al Qaeda network.]

September 1995: The Taliban take Herat [the main city in western Afghanistan.]

September 1996: The Taliban take Jalalabad and Kabul.

1997–1998: The Taliban continue their advances in the north. The city of Mazar-i-Sharif changes hands several times, finally falling to the Taliban in August 1998. [A strategic crossroads only a few miles from the Uzbek border, Mazar-i-Sharif has direct road access to most major Afghan cities, including Taloqan in the east, Kabul in the south, and Herat in the west. Mazar-i-Sharif is alleged to have been the scene of bloody massacres committed both by the Taliban and by forces of the Northern Alliance.]

General Massoud retreats to his home territory in the Panshir Valley and remains the sole effective opponent of the Taliban regime. [The Panshir Valley is an impregnable natural fortress that stretches southwest from northern Afghanistan to the Shamali Plain just north of Kabul.]

September 9, 2001: Ahmed Shah Massoud is the victim of an assassination plot; his death is officially confirmed on September 13.

September 11, 2001: The World Trade Center in New York City and the Pentagon in Washington, D.C. are attacked by terrorists in hijacked commercial airlines. The World Trade Center collapses. The hijackers are believed to be members of Osama bin Laden's Al-Qaeda organization.

October 7, 2001: The beginning of the Anglo-American intervention in Afghanistan.

November 9, 2001: After a month-long American campaign of bombing, the Northern Alliance regains control of Mazar-i-Sharif.

November 13, 2001: The Taliban abandon Kabul overnight; forces of the Northern Alliance enter the capital.

December 22, 2001: Hamid Karzai is sworn in as the leader of an interim government, as agreed in talks held in Bonn, Germany, earlier that month. The coalition is endorsed by Mohammed Zahir Shah, and its thirty members include representatives of several Afghan factions. Karzai is the first person to take power in Afghanistan peacefully in thirty years.